Acclaim for Five Approaches to Philosophy

"Here is a book written with a notable lucidity, characterized by wisdom and tolerance, and remarkable for the range and comprehensiveness of its survey."

"It is the work of a philosopher generous in his sympathies, discerning in his understanding, and fair and frank in his criticisms. Besides the many merits which the book possesses as a particular study, I see it also as yet another symbol of East and West in a fruitful philosophical partnership."

— *Prof. I.T. Ramsey, University of Oxford.*

"I found it most interesting and informative and very clearly expressed."

— *Prof. C.D. Broad, University of Cambridge.*

"I congratulate you on its excellent content and clarity of exposition."

— *Prof. John Wisdom, University of Cambridge.*

"It shows real independent thought."

— *Prof. A.R.Wadia, University of Bombay.*

"It is a contribution to philosophical thinking."

— *Prof. N.A. Nikam, University of Mysore.*

"It is a philosophical work of extraordinary merit, combining lucidity and profundity."

— *Prof. Prem Nath, University of Punjab.*

2nd Edition With Two New Essays

FIVE APPROACHES TO PHILOSOPHY

Auguste Rodin, sculpted *The Thinker* in 1880 in France. Replicas in all sizes now adorn parks, museums, gardens and bookshelves all over the world.

Also by Jamal Khwaja

- Living The Quran In Our Times
- Quest for Islam
- Authenticity and Islamic Liberalism
- The Call of Modernity And Islam
- Essays on Cultural Pluralism
- The Vision of an Unknown Indian
- Numerous articles and scholarly essays

To learn more about the author, visit:

WWW.JAMALKHWAJA.COM

Download free Digital Books, Lectures, Essays and more.

2nd Edition With Two New Essays

FIVE APPROACHES TO PHILOSOPHY

A discerning philosopher philosophizes about the philosophy of philosophy with wisdom and clarity

by

JAMAL KHWAJA

Formerly Professor of Philosophy
Aligarh Muslim University

With a Foreword by

I. T. RAMSEY

Nolloth Professor of Philosophy
Of the Christian Religion
University of Oxford

Alhamd Publishers, LLC
Los Angeles

2nd Edition With Two New Essays

Copyright © by Jamal Khwaja 1965, 2012, 2016

All rights reserved. Copyright under Berne Copyright Convention, Universal Copyright Convention, and Pan American Copyright Convention. No part of this book may be reproduced, stored in a retrieval system, or transmitted in any form or by any means, electronic or mechanical or otherwise, including photocopying and recording, without prior written permission of the publisher, except for the inclusion of brief quotations in a review.
For permission to reproduce selections from this book contact the Publisher.

Published and distributed worldwide by

ALHAMD Publishers, LLC.
3131 Roberts Avenue, Culver City, CA 90232, USA.

www.AlhamdPublishers.com

Printed and bound in the United States of America
Book and Jacket Design by Sandeep Sandhu.
Author Photo by Kenny Zepeda

More information about the Author and his works can be found at

www.JamalKhwaja.com.
Look for FREE Downloads of Essays & Articles written by the Author.

ISBN-13: 978-1-935293-51-4 (Trade Paperback)
Publisher SAN #: 857-0132
BISAC Subject Headings: Philosophy / Methodology (PHI014000)
Philosophy / History & Surveys-Modern (PHI016000)

To my father

Abdul Majid Khwaja,

who is no more to read it

Quotable

Whence? Whither? Why? How? - these questions cover all philosophy.
— *Joseph Joubert*

Philosophy is the peculiarly stubborn attempt to think clearly.
— *William James*

I have gained this by philosophy: that I do without being commanded what others do only from fear of the law.
— *Aristotle*

A little philosophy inclineth men's minds to atheism; but depth in philosophy bringeth men's minds to religion.
— *Bacon*

Contents

AUTHOR'S PREFACE TO THE 2nd EDITION xi

FOREWORD BY PROFESSOR I.T. RAMSEY xiii
AUTHOR'S PREFACE TO THE 1st EDITION xv

Chapter 1: INTRODUCTION 1

Chapter 2: THE RELIGIOUS APPROACH TO PHILOSOPHY 9
General Introduction
The Nature of the Religious Approach to Philosophy
The Justification of the Religious Approach
Limitations of the Religious Approach

Chapter 3: THE METAPHYSICAL APPROACH TO PHILOSOPHY 19
General Introduction
The Onto-cosmological Approach
Limitations of The Onto-cosmological Approach
The Epistemological Approach
Limitations of The Epistemological Approach
The Dialectical Approach
Conclusion

Chapter 4: THE CULTURAL APPROACH TO PHILOSOPHY 33
General Introduction
Delineation of the Cultural Approach
The Changing Patterns of Worldviews
Worldviews and Truth
The Criteria of Validity of Worldviews
Conclusion

Chapter 5: THE ANAYLYTICAL APPROACH TO PHILOSOPHY 51
General Introduction
The Philosophical Analysis of Moore and Russell
Limitations of Logical Atomism & Directional Analysis
The Logical Positivist Approach
Limitations of The Logical Positivist Approach
Linguistic Analysis
The Relation between Moore and Wittgenstein
Limitations of The Linguistic Approach
Phenomenological Analysis
Limitations of Phenomenological Analysis

Chapter 6: THE EXISTENTIALIST APPROACH TO PHILOSOPHY 83
General Introduction
Kierkegaard and Christian Existentialism
The Agnostic Existentialist Approach of Jaspers
The Ontological Existentialism of Heidegger and Sartre
Conclusion

Chapter 7: CONCLUSION 101

Essay 1: Knowledge and Truth 109

Essay 2: A Linguistic Analysis of the Problem of Sense Perception .. 123

Appendix 1: About The Author 141

Appendix 2: Select Bibliography 143

Index 149

Authors Preface to 2ⁿᴰ Edition, 2012

The text of the original 1965 edition has not been altered, much as I would have liked to revise the work. My only justification for shirking this task is that there has been no shift in my philosophical perspective and method. The work was very well received in philosophical circles in India and abroad. Many eminent thinkers made highly favorable comments. However, I have inserted two papers in an appendix. The first is my unpublished paper, ***A Linguistic Analysis of the Problem of Sense Perception***. To my mind, it is a good practical example of linguistic analysis in action. Linguistic Analysis, after all, is a tool for clarifying general ideas, views and also philosophical theories.

The second paper, ***Knowledge and Truth***, was originally included in Balasubramanian and Bhattacharyya, (Ed.) *Freedom, Progress and Society*, 1986, a volume of essays published in honor of the eminent Indian philosopher, Prof. Satchidananda Murty of Tirupati University. This paper is a good example of my multi-dimensional approach to the problem of knowledge and truth. The addition of these two papers should considerably enhance whatever be the value of the first edition of my work.

Jamal Khwaja
Los Angeles,
July 2011

FOREWORD

I am very happy indeed to write a forward to this first book by my old friend and pupil, Mr. Jamal Khwaja, who worked with me years ago in Cambridge. He has written a book which combines the two gifts for which I still remember him from those earlier days - an ability for clear, critical thinking on the one hand, on the other hand a sensitivity and insight which enable him to avoid superficiality - whether the over-facile generalization or the all too confident criticism. Like all good philosophizing, this book reveals the man who has written it.

In his discussion of the notable Cambridge philosopher, G. E. Moore, and having in mind particularly Moores defense of commonsense, Mr. Khwaja reminds us that there will always be scientific assertions about the world which every philosopher must take for granted and certainly never deny. Philosophy is no competing super-science, but rather teaches an approach to the world expressed in terms of a large-scale conceptual pattern. It is five such patterns which this book describes in its '*Metaphilosophy*', that is, its philosophizing about philosophy; the religious approach, the metaphysical approach, the cultural approach, the analytical approach and the existentialist approach. There are sympathetic statements of each approach, and this is followed by paragraphs of discerning criticism, which set out the particular limitations of each. The whole discussion is clear, concise and to the point. Nor is there any of the dangers of an over-simplified classification. Mr. Khwaja recognizes, for instance, that there has often been an interweaving of the religious (or authoritarian) approach and the metaphysical approach: that Hegel combined the metaphysical and cultural approaches; that Heidegger and Sartre combined the existentialist approach with the ontological. Again, he is careful to distinguish between the various different approaches that share the title of '*analytical*'.

On a number of occasions there are several illuminating comparisons. For instance, the difference between Moore and Russell in their approach to Metaphysics is compared to that between Jaspers and Marcel on the

Foreword

one hand, and Heidegger and Sartre on the other. His broad conclusion is that the philosophers perspective on the world must always combine the critical and the sympathetic. It must strive for that clarificatory precision which is the ideal of the analyst, but it must also do justice to all our insights into the human situation. The philosopher must never sponsor a super-scientific metaphysics. Yet neither must he be an irrationalist who despairs of reasonable thinking simply because he cannot know everything for certain. It is such reflections that lead Mr. Khwaja to discuss the possibility of what he calls a multidimensional approach.

Here is a book written with a notable lucidity, characterized by wisdom and tolerance, and remarkable for the range and comprehensiveness of its survey. It is the work of a philosopher generous in his sympathies, discerning in his understanding, and fair and frank in his criticism. Besides the many merits which the book possesses as a particular study, I see it also as yet another symbol of the growing together of East and West in a fruitful philosophical partnership.

Oriel College, Oxford.　　　　　　　　　　　　　　　　Ian T. Ramsey
March, 1965

Author's Preface To The 1ST Edition

This monograph attempts to describe the different, approaches to philosophy, their situational and conceptual fields, their inter-relations and limitations. The possibility of combining them into, a multi-dimensional approach is also discussed.

The key notion underlying this essay is that the actual doing of philosophy must be rooted in a critical and comparative meta-philosophy. Most philosophers are so busy in establishing truths, or analyzing words and sentences, as the case may be, that they tend to neglect meta-philosophy. This leads to methodological isolationism and a polemical instead of an irenic approach to philosophical problems.

No detailed exposition or criticism of theories or problems arising within an approach has been attempted. My dominant concern has been with the structure of approaches and the delineation of their leitmotif, as it were rather than with their immanent problems. I believe it is essential to see how the entire philosophical scene changes with a change in our meta-philosophical perspective, that is, our conception of the nature and task of philosophy. Historical details concerning the origin and development of these approaches are obviously far from complete. Indeed some portions pre-suppose some acquaintance with the development of Western philosophy. In any case, historical completeness would have meant a much bigger work, especially when a number of approaches were being examined. I am conscious of the limitations of the essay, especially the relative paucity of illustrative material. But it is the best I could produce for the present.

I have learnt from so many sources that an adequate acknowledgment of my debts is impossible. I must, however, indicate my great debt to my former teachers at Cambridge, Professor C.D. Broad, Professor John Wisdom and Professor I.T. Ramsey (now of Oxford), and also to Professor G. Ryle and some other distinguished British analytical philosophers. I

Preface

am indebted to J.O. Urmson's, *Philosophical Analysis* and G.J. Warnok's, *English Philosophy Since 1900*, for their lucid treatment of Logical Atomism and Moore's philosophical analysis respectively.

I have also been deeply stimulated by John Dewey as would be evident from the chapter entitled, *The Cultural Approach to Philosophy*. But I have not tried to confine myself to any one philosopher; I must also express my gratitude to Professor Dr. J. Ritter of the University of Munster.

I must thank Professor Habib for his intellectual stimulation in my early life, and my father-in-law, General Mohammad Akbar, for breaking my inner resistance to writing.

Finally, I thank my friends, Mr. Rajendra Singh, Mr. Asoke Chatterjee, Mr. Jamil Qadri and Professor K.A. Nizami for their interest in my work, and last but not least, Professor N.V. Banerjee for his kindness in going through the typescript and giving valuable suggestions.

Aligarh   A. Jamal Khwaja
6th April, 1965

CHAPTER 1

INTRODUCTION

Every science has its distinctive subject matter, and deals with certain fundamental concepts and questions. These constitute its main body. But every science also raises or suggests certain fundamental problems about the nature of its theories, methods of investigation, criteria of truth, limits of validity or inter-relations with other sciences, etcetera. Sometimes both types of problems are treated by the same individual to a greater or lesser extent. But in the case of the natural sciences, the scientist is so absorbed in the laborious activity of factual investigation, and the formulation and testing of hypotheses, that he has little time or energy left to devote to the methodological questions, constituting the philosophy of that science, or the particular meta-science. This convenient division of labor is, however, not feasible in the case of philosophy. Meta-problems concerning the nature and method of philosophy are much more crucial than the meta-problems of natural sciences. Sciences would work, even if a particular philosophy of science were invalid. But a philosophy would, be completely vitiated if its philosophy of philosophy were invalid.

The question I wish to consider, is whether philosophy too has two types of questions, whether there is or ought to be a meta-philosophy or philosophy of philosophy, (just as there is a philosophy of science, philosophy of history, or of mathematics etcetera), as distinct from philosophy. Or ought philosophy itself to perform this function? If so, meta-philosophy would be a redundant expression like logical logic or chemical chemistry etcetera. The nomenclature is trivial, provided, the significance of the distinction is grasped. If meta-questions of philosophy are made an integral part of philosophy, getting their due share of the philosophers attention, then there is no need for coining a new expression.

What has been the past record of philosophy in this respect? Not long ago philosophers were eager to offer systems and neat isms, claiming to be objectively and universally true. Meta-questions were not given their due share of importance, even though they could not he totally avoided. It is significant, that the greater the depth of the philosopher, the greater was his relative concern with them. Thus Plato, Aristotle, Spinoza, Descartes, Locke, Hume, all dealt with these meta-problems, to a greater or lesser degree. But the most notable name is that of Kant.

The trend of the development of Western philosophy has been from an implicit meta-philosophy to an explicit one. This trend is logical and inevitable. A meta-science presupposes a body of sciences, as grammar presupposes language or languages, and philosophy of religion presupposes religions. meta-philosophy presupposes not merely a philosophy but philosophies. Thus even though every great philosopher has also been to some extent or other, a meta-philosopher (the parallel does not hold for scientists); an explicit meta-philosophy could not arise until the problem of philosophical diversity had emerged. Continuing philosophical controversy in the midst of ever growing agreement in other areas of human activity further pinpointed the issue. Consequently Western thought grew to be shy of metaphysics and was oriented towards meta-philosophy. This was not poverty of thought or the drying up of creative thinking. It only reflected a fresh creative response to the contemporary situation, and the emergence of a new conceptual field.

There have been two crucial formative periods of meta-philosophy; the first was the period of the emergence of natural science and scientific method in Europe in the 16th century; the second was the period of the rapid development of natural, social and cultural sciences in the 19th century. The first situation had stimulated a new critical approach to philosophy, distinguishing, though not totally separating, it from scholastic thought. The second epoch made man for the first time systematically conscious of the diversity of languages, art forms, morals, religions, and world views etcetera, in all their richness and depth. This too acted as a leaven for the formulation of fresh questions concerning the nature and relationship of philosophy to the concrete cultural and historical situation of man.

The development of meta-philosophy has taken different directions among Anglo-American and European philosophers. Generally speaking, the first have concerned themselves more or less exclusively with problems generated by the impact of natural science, e.g., problems of meaning, verification, disagreement, truth, and relationship with science etcetera. European philosophers, on the other hand, have been deeply influenced by the impact of the social and cultural sciences.

Anglo-American meta-philosophy tends to locate the striking feature of philosophical disagreement in the scientific frame of reference or conceptual field. In brief the explanation is that philosophical disagreement is the product of a lack of clarity and precision in the concepts and statements of philosophers, or confusion about the various uses of words or types of discourse etcetera. Scientific statements, and specialized languages of logic, mathematics, Physics, are extolled as the ideal and the philosopher is pressed to imitate them. Analysis in one form or the other is held to be the means for achieving clarity. Moore, Russell, Wittgenstein, and the *Logical Positivists* represent this trend.

The German version of meta-philosophy has been different. It highlights the cultural determinants of philosophical theories and of philosophical disagreement. Philosophical statements and theories are sought to be correlated, with the situational matrix of man. This leads to a cultural approach to philosophy. Nietzsche, Marx, Dilthey, Scheler, and Dewey adopt this approach in varying degrees.

Meta-philosophy emerged in response to the challenges posed by philosophical disagreement. Its task was to show why this disagreement existed and how it could be overcome, But it is significant that it itself became a prey to disagreement. Why did this happen? I believe that this was due to a mono-dimensional approach to the problem of the nature of philosophy and the reasons of philosophical disagreement. Philosophers took selected instances of philosophizing as the Paradigm or model of philosophy as such. Similarly, selected instances of philosophical disagreement were made the basis of formulating particular theories of disagreement. It is not surprising that when the Paradigm instances differed, the corresponding meta-philosophical theories of the nature of philosophy and of philosophical disagreement also clashed. Thus the differences, between Anglo-American and European meta-philosophy are quite understandable. But they are not unavoidable. These approaches are not contrary but complementary.

Before proceeding to describe these approaches in the main body of this essay, a few remarks on the cultural determinants of philosophical problems, and the cardinal features of the contemporary situation would be in order.

Philosophical questions and problems are situationally evoked and are not the product of a philosophers ingenuity or reasoning alone. The latter, however, are necessary for articulating his response to the evocative stimulus of the concrete historical situation of the philosopher. Thus, varying life situations lead to the formulation of varying problems. For example, in the Middle Ages it was generally held that nothing happened without the will of God. Since it was also held that God rewarded and punished man, the problems of the freedom of the will and the justification of punishment emerged. Similarly, the problem of pain and evil was generated due to the current beliefs that (a) God is omnipotent and merciful, (b) pain and evil ought not to exist at all, or at least not in the measure in which they actually do in the universe. If either of the above judgments is modified or abandoned, the problem disintegrates. The problem arose precisely because of and within a concrete conceptual and valuational field or situation. A change in this field leads to a change in the problem.

Introduction

Consider the question: Has God created the universe? The once obvious answer was either a categorical yes/no, or a suspension of judgment. But philosophers now accept the possibility and even the validity of a third answer, namely: It all depends upon what you mean by *'God'* and *'creation'* etcetera. There is no one answer. The nature of philosophical problems thus depends upon the cultural climate, the manifold of assumptions within which the philosopher operates, and the concrete historical situation.

Mannheim refers to the situational determination of thought. But the situation evokes rather than determines thought. The significant features of the situation arrest the attention of the sensitive philosopher, while others fail to notice them or grasp their significance. People are thus not compelled by the situation to adopt a certain mode of thought or conceptual field. Rather they are stimulated by the situation as also by their own sensitiveness. Consider a stable social group suddenly brought into conflict with a radically different culture group. Once effective communication has been established, the critical and non-dogmatic thinkers, if any, of both the groups would be led by the logic of the situation to pose inter-cultural macroscopic problems in the place of intra-cultural microscopic ones. A powerful challenge would be thrown to the traditional conceptual field itself, within which the problems, agreements and disagreements had their being. Instead of raising questions like; Can God change the past? Or, Are His attributes separable or not from His Essence? Can He commit evil? Or Are Forms and Ideas (of Plato) immanent or transcendent? Etcetera. Or, in an entirely different context, does a table continue to exist when not perceived by any mind? Do other minds exist? What is the relation between sense data and objects? Etcetera. Some philosophers would be powerfully inclined to raise questions like: How do different problems arise? Why does philosophical disagreement exist? What is the nature and function of philosophical theories? What is the correct method of approach to philosophical problems? Etcetera.

What type of problem engages the philosopher depends upon his personality type and the degree of his ability to detach himself from the conceptual field and manifold of assumptions of his age and group. If, however, he fails to appreciate the logic of the situational evocation of problems, and clings to a superseded conceptual field, then his philosophy does not grip the contemporary mind.

Granting that philosophical problems change with changing conditions, are there no stable sets of questions constituting its proper domain? I believe that the only stable and permanent questions are meta-questions. Meta-philosophy remains, while philosophies, come and go. If Plato and Kant, Ghazzali and Ibn Rushd, Shanker and Vallabh, still interest us, it is because they are either meta-philosophers, or there is a point of contact between our conceptual fields and theirs.

The present human situation is characterized by scientific uniformity and progress in the midst of philosophical controversy and religious and cultural diversity. This is perhaps the most significant feature of the contemporary situation. This generates the basic conceptual field for the critically oriented contemporary philosopher. It may be called the meta-philosophical field. Methodological, questions like the nature of philosophical, metaphysical, ethical and logical statements, the theories of meaning and truth, the nature and dynamics of philosophical or ethical controversy etcetera, arise within this field. Controversy and disagreement in the midst of progressively expanding scientific and technological standardization appear as anachronisms to the contemporary mind. It is impelled to find the causes and the cure of this incongruity. This leads to an unprecedented interest in meta-problems of almost all the branches of knowledge.

The value judgment underlying this quest is that avoidable controversy or conflict is bad and must be overcome. The contemporary analytical and meta-philosophical approaches are the new instruments to serve this basic value, even as previous metaphysical systems were the instruments of serving and defending some value system or other, embedded in past cultural traditions. In other words, harmony or agreement is the motif of contemporary meta-philosophy.

Introduction

It may be said that this is the motif of all philosophy and religion as such. This is probably true. But the range of harmony sought by contemporary philosophers is immensely wider than the range previously sought. Moreover, there is a distinction between a democratic harmony among autonomous individuals freely committing themselves to values, and the harmony that ensues as a result of the commitment to an external *Authority*. No doubt the philosophical theologian claims that since his acceptance of the *Authority* is based upon universally valid reasons, the harmony that accrues is rooted in reason rather than a dogmatic or arbitrary surrender to an *Authority*. This claim will be examined in the chapter *The Religious Approach to Philosophy*.

CHAPTER 2

THE RELIGIOUS APPROACH TO PHILOSOPHY

GENERAL INTRODUCTION

The word 'religion' like the words 'justice', 'democracy', 'philosophy', and 'art' etcetera, connotes different things to different people. The concrete meaning ranges from the opium of the people to self-realization, universal love, surrender to the Supreme Creator, absorption in Divinity etcetera. Hence the expression *'religious approach'* is also ambiguous. What I propose to say about the *'religious approach'* to philosophy should not be confused with the religious approach to life, even though these two themes over-lap to a certain degree. The religious approach to life refers to the basic way in which an individual orientates himself to the universe. The *'religious approach'* to philosophy refers to his basic conception of the nature and tasks of philosophy. A person may be deeply religious in one of the various senses of the term, and yet his approach to philosophy may not be religious, but metaphysical or analytical or cultural. For example, Socrates among the ancients, Kant and Spinoza among the moderns, and Karl Jasper's among our contemporaries will be admitted to be religious persons in one of the various senses of the term. But they cannot be said to adopt the *'religious approach'* to philosophy.

It would be going too far from my present purpose to survey the various meanings of the terms *'religion'* and *'religious approach'*.

I shall only explain the exact sense in which the expression *'religious approach'* is being used here, and then point out its basic features and interrelations with other approaches.

The above remarks should not be taken to imply that my adopted use of the expression *'religious approach'* is arbitrary and does not follow common usage. Indeed, it appears to me, that it is precisely in this sense, that the words religion and *'religious approach'* are most commonly used in ordinary speech. Philosophers and others who, whether consciously or subconsciously, advance persuasive definitions of religion use the other senses. The undetected presence of persuasive components in these definitions leads to confusion and controversy. Erich Fromm, for example, divides religion into two broad types; humanistic and authoritarian. This division cuts across the familiar distinction between theistic and non-theistic religions. According to his classification, early Buddhism and early Christianity, Taoism, and the religions of Socrates and Spinoza represented humanistic religion. Since the world view or belief system of say, Spinoza, is quite different from that of Saint Peter, the word *'religion'* is being used in a very wide sense. This is, however, not to criticize Fromm's penetrating insight into the function of religion in the life of man. My purpose is merely to illustrate the extremely wide connotative and denotative spectrum of the word *'religion'* and the persuasive elements implicit in such definitions.

THE NATURE OF THE RELIGIOUS APPROACH TO PHILOSOPHY

What, then, is the nature or, more exactly, the function of the *'religious approach'* to philosophy. Its function is to defend and justify ones commitment to an external *Authority*. At times its function is the systematic rediscovery or reinterpretation of the meaning and implications of a traditional belief system that continues to grip and fascinate the individual. This latter function is nearer to a pure metaphysical or speculative approach. But, in so far as it is limited to reinterpretation of a belief system without an explicit questioning of its basic truth or validity; the activity of speculation is only partly free. Hence this controlled speculative reinterpretation remains distinct from the pure speculative construction of world views or value systems by a fully autonomous individual.

The *'religious approach'* to philosophy is perhaps the oldest and persists even today in many circles of the East and West. At the early stage of human history, the individual, generally speaking, stands committed to an external Authority, who is the source of the value system and the world view commonly accepted by the group. This shared commitment strengthens group solidarity and gives inner peace to the individual. Yet, his desire for comprehensiveness, consistency and logical or aesthetic order and system, impel him to systematize and refine the world view. In the course of this activity, or even prior to it, he may discover certain prima facie inconsistencies in the belief-system or grounds of possible doubt. But this does not weaken his commitment. It induces him to remove those inconsistencies either by pointing out that they are only apparent or through making ad hoc assumptions. Sometimes a considerable reconstruction of concepts and beliefs may be attempted. This task requires conceptual analysis and logical deduction.

There is a second motif for this type of rationalistic activity. For some reason or other, the individuals commitment to his *Authority* may start to waver. Reasoning then plays the role of a doctor curing a patient. Reasoning removes inductively, or deductively, or in a mixed way, doubts about the world view and value system.

Apart from the desire for logical order and consistency for their own sake, there is also the desire to make the value system and world view universally acceptable. The individual is more or less clearly aware of the fact of disagreement between different people or groups. This creates a sense of uneasiness, if not of doubt. It shows the lack of a total harmony between man and man. He wishes to extend the sense of group solidarity to the entire human family. But since others are perhaps committed to some other *Authority*, they can grasp the truth only if it is rationally demonstrable. May be reason by itself is insufficient for grasping the truth, unless aided by some external—source, more potent than reason. However, the individual thinks that the activity of reasoning has its own distinct value, limited though it may be.

Thus the *leitmotif* of the *'religious approach'* to philosophy may be said to be a combination in varying proportions of the desires for logical order, universal acceptance of the belief system and defense against internal or external attack.

The religious and the pure speculative or metaphysical approach are sometimes intertwined. This results in a qualified and controlled speculation or a reversionary adherence to the traditional belief system. Many terms and expressions and also some foundational concepts of the traditional world view and value system are retained. But the creative religious individual gives them a new concrete content. As an instance of a comprehensive conceptual reconstruction, this effort evokes admiration. But from the point of view of orthodox faith, it may be a very misleading activity.

The speculative and the religious or conformist trends may be present in varying degrees in different individuals. The pure conformist approach in total isolation from the speculative is hardly ever to be found in a philosopher. To the extent that this is the case, he becomes a theologian rather than a philosopher.

The dominant trend of ancient Indian philosophy was religious in the sense defined. The Vedas, or the Upanishads, more exactly, the *Sruti* portions, were accepted as infallible or divine in some sense. The task of reflection and reasoning was to grasp their truth and elaborate it systematically. There were, however, non-conformist thinkers from the very beginning, even though in a minority. Even in a purely academic essay like the present one, the tolerance initially shown to these heterodox thinkers of remote antiquity deserves not only mention but also praise.

The Religious Approach to Philosophy

Medieval Christian and Muslim scholasticism reflects the same approach. Philosophy does not question *Authority*. The locus or radius of *Authority* may be narrowed and restricted to the Quran alone, as the Divinely Inspired word of God, or may be more or less widened to include certain utterances of the Holy Prophet. In the case of Christianity the locus of *Authority* may be the Bible as a whole or in parts, or the Church as the body of the Christ.

The *Mutazalite* thinkers of Islam are sometimes regarded as pure rationalists. But their rationalism was not absolute. They never questioned the infallibility of the Quran, although they differed from its traditional interpretation in many matters. Some later Muslim thinkers of Spain and North Africa, particularly Ibn Rushd and Ibn Arabi adopted an approach more metaphysical than religious. They attempted a very radical reconstruction of traditional beliefs and concepts.

The conceptual field of the *'religious approach'* is constituted by the concrete elements of the belief system to which the person is committed, for example, creation, life after death, rebirth, the existence and nature of a *Supreme Being*, revelation, cosmic purpose, etcetera.

These concepts determine the direction of the philosophers thinking. Thus, a Muslim or Christian philosopher raises questions like; Can God change the past? What is the justification of punishment when God is the ultimate Doer? Was creation out of nothing? Are truths of reason binding upon God? What is the purpose of creation? Can a morally good non-believer win salvation? Why is there so much pain and evil in the world? Etcetera.

A Hindu philosopher would pose different questions such as: Why does one normally not remember the events of a previous incarnation? What is the relation between the *Absolute Brahman* and the *Atman*? What is *Maya*? Etcetera.

THE JUSTIFICATION OF THE RELIGIOUS APPROACH

The cultural climate of the modem world makes us all, including the religious person; admit the desirability and value of a rational approach to religion. The profession of an irrevocable blind choice exposes him to the charge of dogmatism. This cultural climate did not always prevail. Even to day in some milieus, the open profession of a dogmatic faith brings recognition to the individual. He takes pride in the intensity and unshaken-ability of his faith. But in the philosophers milieu, a person finds it difficult to admit a blind and irrevocable faith in a book or creed. He is apt to assure both himself and others, that even if, as a matter of fact, he does accept an external *Authority* as infallible, he does so on rational grounds. Some persons might even profess willingness to revise their system of beliefs, if fresh evidence were to demand or compel such revision. In short, they claim that their commitment to the infallible *Authority* is rational. But can such a commitment be entirely rational? Or can the infallibility of the *Authority* be proved? This is the crux of the problem. It must be admitted, that if the infallibility could be proved, the commitment, if made, could rightfully claim to be rational, in the strict sense.

How can the infallibility of the *Authority* be proved? It can be proved only by showing an invariable agreement between the judgments of the *Authority*, and those judgments of the individual that result from the most careful investigation and reflection. But what is the guarantee that this activity represents his authentic decisions, and reasons, without his being influenced by the valuations and prescriptions of the *Authority*, with whom he may already be acquainted. May it not be, that the will to conform predisposes him to accept the value judgments of the *Authority*, as if they were his own authentic ones? He considers the bare fact of agreement or coincidence between the two as a proof of the infallibility of the *Authority*. But this is no proof. However, if an honest claim of full agreement in all examined cases is made, we will have to accept that the faith of the individual in the infallibility of the *Authority* is just like any other inductive conclusion. This means that it could be a rational faith.

It may, however, turn out that there is a conflict between the judgments of the individual and the *Authority*. This is a crucial matter. If the individual agrees even in a single instance of such conflict, that his judgment is wrong because his intelligence is limited, and that the judgment of the *Authority* must he right or valid, because it is infallible, then this belief in its infallibility is no longer an inductively established or rational belief. It is nothing more and nothing less than plain and simple faith, or commitment.

This, however, does not mean that such faith is irrational. If a thing or judgment is not rational, this does not mean that it is irrational. It may be partly rational and partly non-rational, or it may even have irrational elements intertwined with the rational. A simple two-valued logic of rational/irrational is not applicable here. The phenomenon of personal love provides an illuminating analogy. Can the state of being in deep love with a person, say, a great leader or artist be a fully rational attitude, or can deliberate detachment he accepted as fully irrational? Obviously such issues or questions are not amenable to a simple either/or logic. Falling in deep love is neither a rational nor an irrational action.

It may be objected that the above procedure is methodologically vitiated, since it makes the admittedly fallible human judgment the criterion of the validity of the judgments of the *Infallible Authority*. This objection is hardly respectable. It is precisely the infallibility of the *Authority* that is required to be proved. It cannot be assumed. If it is assumed, then the claim of the commitment to be rational is *ipso facto* given up. But if it is to be proved, the proof must, by the very nature of the case, rely upon human reasoning as the final criterion of validity. No doubt, the possibility of error would always be present. But there is a measure of risk, however infinitesimal, in all human reasoning beyond the sphere of logico-mathematical inference.

If a person accepts an *Authority* as infallible then he must accept the logical consequence of this choice for the pursuit of philosophy. The logical consequence is the abandonment of intellectual autonomy, and the moral as well as logical obligation to conform to the *Authority* in all ones judgments. The choice is between commitment and autonomy. Philosophy cannot dictate the choice. But up to a point reasons may be given for accepting one or the other, in terms of the consequences of the two attitudes. It is essentially a moral choice between two irreconcilable values. Both commitment and autonomy are basic values with a strong appeal. What is important is that the nature of the alternative values and their consequences must be clear to the individual. He can integrate his personality and become a productive and happy individual in either way. It is up to the individual to make this foundational decision, assuming that he is not already in the deep and powerful grip of some *Authority*. But if he does commit himself to an *Authority*, then he will have to give up the philosophical activity understood as a free and uncommitted search for truth or validity, a quest without strings, a journey without a pre-established destination, a pursuit without the guarantee of eternal certitude.

He may pursue philosophy in the sense of systematic apologetics. But these two conceptions of philosophy are poles apart. It is important in this context to distinguish the limited freedom of interpretation and the reasoning involved in immanent analysis and exegesis from the theoretically unlimited autonomy of the pure philosopher.

The above analysis is not concerned with the merits of any claim or claims that some *Authority* is infallible. It only aims to analyze the logic of such claims and the methodology of the *'religious approach'* to philosophy rather than religion as such. The conclusion is that the *'religious approach'* to philosophy is incompatible with the intellectual autonomy of man. This is a truism. But some times the reiteration of truisms is necessary and illuminating.

LIMITATIONS OF THE RELIGIOUS APPROACH TO PHILOSOPHY

This approach satisfies only those persons whose commitment to an *Authority* does not generate any inner conflict. Such a smooth commitment occurs when the demands of the deeper authentic personality and value structure of the individual harmonize or correspond with the underlying temper or spirit of the *Authority*, rather than merely with its specific prescriptions etcetera. In such cases a pre-established harmony or affinity may be said to exist between the *Authority* and the individual. But where this is absent, the *'religious approach'* does not lead to an authentic peace that passeth understanding. In spite of commitment to the *Authority*, silent notes of discord mar the inner harmony of the committed person. If such a person seeks the help of philosophy then the fully critical approach to philosophy instead of the *'religious approach'* with its limited freedom, is more likely to still the notes of discord.

The *'religious approach'* to philosophy is obviously a partly closed or sealed approach. The total or partial non-recognition of this fact leads to considerable confusion about the nature of philosophy and the philosophical attitude and method. The secondary rationalistic activity and immanent analysis of the philosophical theologian is liable to be confused with the primary rationalistic activity, and transcendental analysis of the philosopher.

Man today lives in a multi-cultural rather than a mono-cultural society. Value systems and world views compete among themselves for his allegiance. The *'religious approach'* to philosophy is not critical enough to satisfy contemporary man, once the awareness of the plurality of *Authorities* severs or even loosens the sacred bond of commitment to his traditional *Authority*.

CHAPTER 3

THE METAPHYSICAL APPROACH TO PHILOSOPHY

GENERAL INTRODUCTION

The expression metaphysical approach can be used in different senses. In the strictest sense, metaphysics means *Ontology* or the theory of *Being* or *Reality*. But it has been so closely connected with epistemology or the theory of knowledge that the two must be taken together. The widest sense of the expression metaphysical approach would, however, cover the cultural approach as well, which is a reformed version of the traditional metaphysical approach to philosophy. Metaphysics is as old as philosophy itself. Though in some senses of the term, it has become moribund, in other senses it continues to flourish vigorously in many quarters.

The metaphysical approach is evoked by two powerful human impulses. The first is the impulse to carry the foundational distinction of appearance and reality to its limit, once the common sense realistic view of the world and of knowledge has been questioned. The second is the impulse to construct a comprehensive theory of the nature, origin and future of the world as a whole, including man himself. In an important sense, the scientific approach is also concerned with precisely the same questions. But there is a basic difference between the two. This will be clarified as we proceed. The *'religious approach'* to philosophy also deals with the nature, past and future of the universe.

But it is confined to the elaboration and explication of an infallible belief-cum-value system. This task requires considerable deductive reasoning and the speculative reconstruction of the traditional belief and value system, as already indicated in the previous chapter. But the *'religious approach'* to philosophy does not permit a completely free exploration of the theories about the nature, past and future of the universe. It permits immanent but not transcendental speculation. The metaphysical approach questions the foundations of the framework itself no less than the concrete content of the belief system.

Let us consider the basic distinction between *Reality* and appearance referred to above. This distinction is not posited by the philosopher, as in the case of minute technical distinctions, but is as universally embedded in human thinking as the distinction between subject and object, the self and the other, or the good and the bad. This distinction is suggested by the ordinary day-to-day perceptual experience of man. The concepts of *Reality* and appearance are initially empirical ones, and are employed at the level of common sense. But human thinking does not stop here. It develops into scientific thought on the one hand, and metaphysical speculation on the other. Natural science is based upon a highly systematic and precise form of ordinary perceptual knowledge. It seeks to know the real nature and laws of things and events, as distinguished from their apparent nature. But the word *'real'* is still used in science in an empirical context. That is, *Reality* refers to *Reality* as it appears to human observers under controlled, specific and repeatable conditions of perception. This means that scientific knowledge is relative to the human observer. Man, however, yearns for absolute knowledge of *Reality* as it is in itself, and not merely as it appears to him under controlled conditions. Metaphysical speculation is an attempt to satisfy this deep urge.

There is yet another reason for such speculation. Scientific knowledge is piecemeal and fragmentary. Different sciences either deal with different areas of the universe or adopt different key concepts for explaining it. But man wants a synoptic and integrated knowledge of the universe as a whole. To the extent that science becomes a synoptic and integrated survey of the universe, or a conceptual explanatory scheme embracing the totality of existence, it serves a philosophical or metaphysical purpose. It is significant that, though the metaphysical concept of *Reality* is more radical and far-reaching than the scientific concept, the metaphysical enterprise started much earlier than the scientific enterprise of systematically describing and explaining *Reality* in the empirical sense. There are at least two explanations of this sequence. Firstly, the scientific enterprise is a very patient, piecemeal and long drawn out process. It also requires technological skill, which in turn requires pure science. Minute observations and complicated experiments were not possible at the early stage of human history. The metaphysical enterprise needed no such paraphernalia. Moreover, it promised, quick, certain, exciting and comprehensive results. It, therefore, appealed to man.

Secondly, the metaphysical enterprise was fresh and novel, and man, in his virginal innocence, was naturally inclined to take its claims at their face value. He was not critical enough to question whether pure a priori speculation could yield certain and universally acceptable conclusions. The philosophical disagreement he encountered was judged to be a temporary phase. He was justifiably optimistic about the metaphysical enterprise. Even his subsequent disillusionments have deterred him only partly from engaging in this activity.

Let us now see in greater detail how the metaphysical use of the distinction between *Reality* and appearance emerges from the common sense or empirical use. Our common sense interprets perceptual experience as direct acquaintance or confrontation with objects existing independently in a spatio-temporal world. But this realism is given a jolt by three considerations. Firstly, perceptual illusion and error show that at least some cases of perception are not direct, and that they do not reveal objects as they are in themselves, but only as they appear to observers. Secondly, the experience of various perspectives of the same object and the realization that the perceptual content is correlated with or relative to the situation of the perceiving subject, destroy the belief in the direct confrontation with objects. Thirdly, the gradual realization of the physiological mechanics of the perceptual process, that is, the laws, conditions and limitations of the working of sense organs also contributes to shake, if not shatter, the natural realism of man.

This suggests that the perceptual content does not depend merely upon the object per se, but depends upon (a) the situation of the object, on the one hand, and (b) the situation and condition of the subject at the time of perception, on the other. Thus, the simplicity, directness or immediacy and the veracity of perceptual knowledge as such are brought into doubt. Which piece of knowledge under which conditions is true knowledge? And which is false? May it not be that all cases of perceptual knowledge are false? May it not be that perceptual knowledge as such, is relative to the nature of the perceiving subject, so that subjects with a different perceptual apparatus would perceive objects in a different fashion? If so, what is the ground for holding that the perceptual content corresponds with the nature of objects as they are in themselves?

It should be noticed that these doubts and questions follow from certain assumptions. The first assumption is that independently existing objects have a determinate nature, independent of the relationship of perceptual cognition between object and subject. The same object cannot be both 'x' and 'not x', or 'y' and 'not y', since this would violate the basic law of non-contradiction. Only one particular perceptual report describes the object as it really is; others describe the object, as it appears to be.

The second assumption is that this determinate nature of objects is independent of the relations of an object with other objects, so that different objects are externally related to each other. Whitehead calls these twin assumptions the '*fallacy of independent location*'. When the essential relativity of perceptual knowledge to the structure and functioning of the perceptual apparatus or perceiving subject is viewed in the light of the above two assumptions, this logically leads to a questioning of the common sense view of perception as a direct confrontation with objects leading to a revelation of their determinate objective nature. The pure *object revealing* or *revelatory conception*, as it were, according to which, perception is a discovery of some entity out there, gives place to a constructional conception of knowledge. According to this, perception is not pure discovery, but a complex process of both discovery and construction on the part of the perceiving subject. If so, how can we, grasp the absolute nature of objects as they are in themselves? Is there any kind of knowledge of the nature of objects as they are in themselves? If there are no means of knowing the nature of objects as they are in themselves, then what is the status and criterion of truth of knowledge available to man? This is how the epistemological-cum-onto-cosmological constellation of problems is generated. There is not one single problem, but a complex or family of interrelated questions. They cannot be answered in isolation, because a particular answer to one question implies a corresponding answer to some other question or questions.

The above delineated conceptual field or frame is the common starting point of the metaphysical approach to philosophy. But from this point onwards, different philosophers follow different routes.

One main route is the onto-cosmological approach; the other is the epistemological approach. The third is the dialectical approach of Hegel. Together they constitute the metaphysical approach in the wider sense of the term.

THE ONTO-COSMOLOGICAL APPROACH

Having grasped the essentially relative character of perceptual knowledge, and consolidated the distinction between sensible appearances and metaphysical *Reality*, the philosophers of this school lose interest in further reflection upon the nature and limits of knowledge, and proceed straight away to an a priori apprehension of the ultimate nature and structure of *Reality*. But this step follows from another assumption. The assumption is that though perceptual knowledge is relative, conceptual knowledge based on pure is absolutely true. This assumption is strengthened due to the certainty and universal agreement characterizing pure mathematics.

Kant criticized this approach as dogmatic. However, once this approach is adopted, a number of onto-cosmological questions emerge, for example, is *Reality* one or more, than one? What is the structure of *Reality*? And what are the laws of its functioning? Has the world been created or has it evolved? Is there any purpose in the world? Etcetera.

Corresponding to the above questions a number of alternative answers are given. These constitute the philosophical theories of Monism, Dualism, Pluralism, Materialism, Idealism, Theism and Mechanism, etcetera. Some of these theories overlap even as the questions do. This necessitates the activity of clarification and analysis, which is inseparable from philosophy, indeed all systematic thought for that matter.

This metaphysical analysis is, however, only a means and not an end, from the standpoint of the metaphysical approach to philosophy. Moreover, the analysis in question is contextual and not meta-textual, or in other words, immanent and not transcendental. It does not analyze the basic conceptual field and the assumptions organically linked with it. It confines the analysis to the questions and answers that arise within the field or context. Thus, the question whether *Reality* is one or more than one, is analyzed or split into the ontological question on the one hand, and the substantive question on the other. The theories of Materialism, Idealism, and Dualism are answers to the ontological question, while the theories of Substantial Monism or Pluralism are answers to the second question. But the question of the validity of the field and the basic assumptions that generated these questions is not touched at all by such a metaphysical analysis. However, there is no sharp and rigid demarcation between contextual and meta-textual analysis. The former tends to develop into the latter, particularly if the philosopher is sensitive to the linguistic and situational determinants of the problems of philosophy.

The Metaphysical Approach to Philosophy

LIMITATIONS OF THE ONTO-COSMOLOGICAL APPROACH

The discrepancies between pure speculative accounts of *Reality* pose a problem, even as perceptual diversity and relativity do about the status of perceptual knowledge. It is the problem of the nature and criteria of the truth of metaphysical theories.

The traditional solution was that the account given by the philosopher himself was the only true or objective account. Other philosophers were mistaken, not having *seen* or *grasped* the truth. Philosophical controversy or disagreement would end, if they reflected more carefully and dispassionately, and were more sensitive to the inconsistencies that exist in their own systems. The true account as advanced by the philosopher himself would ultimately receive universal and final acceptance. The progress of factual or empirical knowledge was irrelevant to its final truth, since empirical knowledge concerns phenomena and not *Noumena*.

This is obviously a very crude and unsatisfactory answer to a key question. Both the cultural and the analytical approaches try to give a more satisfactory answer.

The onto-cosmological approach views the reasoning faculty are a fixed and ready made instrument or rather possession of man. It does not relate the mode of functioning of reason to the situational matrix of man, including his cultural patterns and value system. Nor is the functioning of reason correlated with the structure and functioning of the conceptual apparatus or, in Kant's language, with the categories of understanding.

The ontological approach also neglects the analysis of language, even though a certain measure of analysis of concepts or statements is inevitable for philosophy, as indeed for all thinking. This analysis is often vitiated by a lack of a proper theory of meaning and types of discourse, etcetera. The prima facie super-factual statements of metaphysics are, thus, taken at their face value, and confused with persuasive definitions, or a reconstruction of a traditional language system. Thus, terminological recommendations are confused with a priori discovery of facts.

Perhaps an outstanding example of, what I call, contextual analysis is the analysis of the mind body relationship by Broad in his book, *Mind and its Place in Nature*. He mentions seventeen theories, and analyses them with a view to ascertaining the true or correct theory. Such analysis is critical but not critical enough for a meta-philosophically oriented approach. This type of analysis does not question the validity of the conceptual field, which generates the analysandum, that is, the concepts, or statements that are analyzed. It limits itself to definition, classification and reconstruction of concepts and statements with a view to the removal of inconsistencies or inadequacies in a comprehensive system of beliefs. It certainly removes much confusion. But it fails to remove the more subtle ones that result from hidden assumptions about the nature of language and of philosophical statements.

A meta-textual analysis, on the other hand, is analysis at a deeper level. The linguistic analysis of the ordinary language type or the situational analysis implicit in the cultural approach to philosophy, are different versions of meta-textual or transcendental analysis, in my sense of the word.

THE EPISTEMOLOGICAL APPROACH

This approach refuses to follow the ontological route, until a more rigorous and comprehensive theory of the nature, kinds, limits and validity of knowledge has been formulated. Plato and all the modern philosophers since Descartes, accept this approach. But Kant is the critical epistemologist par excellence. Instead of uncritically accepting the superior cognitive status of pure a priori knowledge vis a vis perceptual knowledge, he examines the claim of a priori conceptual knowledge to be absolutely and objectively true. He concludes that

The Metaphysical Approach to Philosophy

conceptual knowledge is no less relative to the forms of human understanding, than is perceptual knowledge to the forms of human perception. Thus, metaphysics or onto-cosmology as an objective super-science in declared to be impossible.

The analysis of the nature of mathematical knowledge played a crucial role in Kant's approach. Although Descartes was a mathematician himself, and Spinoza deliberately followed the geometrical model in his *Ethics*, they did not give sufficient importance to the question of its nature, and its significance for a theory of knowledge, as had been done by Plato. Reichenbach remarks in his *The Rise of Scientific Philosophy*, that Plato's theory of *Ideas* was essentially his mode of answering how mathematics was possible. Leaving apart Leibniz's clear formulation of the distinction between analytic and synthetic judgments, it was Kant who, for the first time after Plato, made the study of the nature of mathematics the key, not only to the epistemological problem, but the onto-cosmological as well.

The conceptual field of the epistemological approach is, thus, generated by giving central and crucial importance to the cognitive aspect of human experience, or to knowledge in general. It raises the questions of the ultimate nature, structure and laws of knowing, rather than of the object of knowledge. The ontological approach questions the common sense epistemological realism, which we all accept before the stage of philosophical sophistication is reached. But it does not question the theoretically possible relativity or relational character of pure rational knowledge itself. The epistemological approach is not satisfied with such an inadequate theory of knowledge. It protests that the ontological enterprise cannot proceed, as if, it were the essence and core of philosophical activity, while all else were marginal.

The epistemological approach leads to the following conceptions of the limits of knowledge.

(a) We may be led into some form of Positivism or other. In an important sense Kant was a positivist. But for his regulative Ideas of

Pure Reason, and the postulates of morality or moral experience, he is almost as anti-metaphysical in his approach as the *Logical Positivists*

(b) The acceptance of a total skepticism or agnosticism accompanied by a helpless lamentation over our fate.

(c) The acceptance of some mode of apprehension other than rational reflection as doing adequately what reason does inadequately, namely, the revelation of the nature of *Reality* as it is in itself. Intuition and mystical experience may then be elevated to the coveted status of an ontological guide.

Let us first consider the claim of intuition or mystical experience to have exclusive access to the *sanctum sanctoras* of core of *Reality*. Mystical experience is also a process. It cannot be conclusively proved or shown that mystical experience does hot distort or refract the nature of *Reality*. The type and range of refraction may differ from perceptual refraction on the one hand, and conceptual refraction, on the other. No matter what its nature, the possibility of refraction as a result of the peculiar modes of mystical experience cannot be ruled out. Hence, the ghost of skepticism is not exorcised.

Secondly, the acceptance of the superior cognitive status of mystical experience does not solve the problem of conflict or disagreement about the nature of *Reality*. The reports given by different mystics vary as much as the perceptual reports of different observers or even the same observer at different times. Which mystic is true or reliable and why? Either the validity of mystical reports has to be established through normal methods involving investigation and reflection, or the problem of validity or truth remains unsolved. The first alternative deprives mystical experience of its alleged superior cognitive status; the second leads to an anarchy of claims and counter-claims to reveal the nature of *Absolute Reality*.

The second alternative of complete skepticism is patently unacceptable to the vast majority of human beings. Cognitive and ethical

The Metaphysical Approach to Philosophy

Nihilism is perhaps self-contradictory and certainly unacceptable. The accompanying lamentation over a helpless skepticism betrays that we have fallen into a '*type*' mistake. All knowledge is essentially rational and contextual. To lament over this is as uncalled for as the lamentation that we can not answer whether numbers are honest or dishonest, or that we cannot experience the pain of others etcetera.

The positivist alternative appears to be the only sound and valid one. It gives up the distinction between knowledge of *Noumena* and knowledge of Phenomena. This does not amount to the abolishing of the dichotomy objective/subjective or *Reality*/appearance within the field of human experience. The real rose has color Red_1, but it appears as Red_2, Red_3, and Red_4, etcetera, to different observers, or the same observer under different conditions. Kant emphatically distinguished sensible reality from sensible appearance. But he held that sensible reality should not be confused with *Noumena* or *Noumenal Reality*. Thus, he after all went beyond *Positivism*. He denied the possibility of metaphysics. But he did not deny the significance of the ontological problem. Whether he was justified in retaining the concept of *Noumena* at all, is not an easy question to answer. Linguistic analysis of the ordinary language type is pertinent to this question and can prove very illuminating. This subject has been dealt with in a later chapter.

LIMITATIONS OF THE EPISTEMOLOGICAL APPROACH

This is more critical than the onto-cosmological approach. But its analysis is mainly contextual as in the previous approach. It also suffers from, the lack of an adequate meta-philosophy and consequently, is unable to eliminate avoidable confusions and disagreements. The conflicting claims of epistemological theories like Intuitionism, Rationalism and Empiricism to be absolutely and exclusively true is a pertinent example of controversy, which is generated by the assimilation of different types of knowledge to one favored Paradigm ease. Traditional epistemology could not resolve the controversy due to its comparative neglect of meta-philosophy. It ignores the question of the genesis of these conflicting theories. Kant's approach is, however, largely, though not entirely, free from those limitations. Finally, the epistemological approach is perhaps a circular or regressive approach. It seeks to assess the limits and status of different types: of knowledge, including pure a priori knowledge. But this assessment is made, indeed has to be made through a priori knowledge or reflection itself. The limits of reason are discovered by or through reasoning itself. But if reason does not give absolute knowledge, then the limits set by reason will not correspond with the objective nature of knowledge. In other words, if we accept that reason supplies us with limited knowledge, then since the knowledge is itself the product of reasoning, this particular conclusion cannot be absolutely true. It will have a limited truth. Thus, a negative and destructive skepticism than mere agnosticism is latent in the epistemological approach. This nihilistic trend or impulse is usually not allowed to show itself, and is suppressed by the epistemological approach. Nihilism is usually repulsive to the vast majority of human beings, including philosophers, since it is the acme of despair.

This is perhaps also the explanation of the radical repudiation of the epistemological approach of Kant by the German romantic philosophers, Fichte and Schelling, and also by Hegel, who formulated the dialectical approach. The overt restrictions and the latent nihilistic tendency of the epistemological approach fail to satisfy the deep and powerful human longing for truth. Philosophers no less than other individuals are powerfully attracted towards an approach that promises the systematic and controlled satisfaction of this longing.

THE DIALECTICAL APPROACH TO PHILOSOPHY

Two approaches are intertwined in Hegel; the abstract logical and the concrete historical or cultural. Hegel's contribution to the formulation of the latter approach is given in the appropriate place. Only the logico-metaphysical or the dialectical approach is considered in this section.

The Metaphysical Approach to Philosophy

Kant had shown that pure a priori reasoning was not pure and passive discovery of what was out there, but a process, which organized the manifold of sensations, and thus partly constructed phenomenal objects of knowledge out of them. He had, thus, excluded *Noumenal Reality* from the range of knowledge. Yet, he posited *Noumena* as the metaphysical ground of sensible appearance. Now to say that *Noumena* were the essential ground of appearance was to say something definite and specific about things in themselves, and, hence, contradicted his own theory of knowledge. Hegel rejected this epistemological approach and this rigid distinction between *Noumena* and phenomena. But he accepted the dynamic functioning of reason, its organizing and synthetic activity. The laws of this activity revealed the nature of things in them selves, rather than of phenomenal objects. The categories of understanding and of reason are also the categories of *Reality*. But these categories do not exist as fixed and ready-made moulds of human reason. Nor do external objects impose them. They develop according to the necessary dialectical laws of the Absolute Spirit of which the individual mind is a reflection.

Thus, the conflict between traditional metaphysical or epistemological theories is uncalled for, as they are necessary stages in, the dialectical development of the World Spirit. The conceptual field of the dialectical approach is, thus, quite distinct from, that of the ontological or epistemological approach. It is constituted by the dialectical movement of thought in a spiral, whose stages are the positing of the thesis, the anti-thesis and the mediating synthesis. The specific problems arising within this approaches are concerned with the proper location of concepts in the dialectical movement, or the identification of the elements of the dialectical triad composing, these concepts, together with pointing out their stage in the dialectical process. The rival philosophical theories are, therefore, neither true nor false, but only more or less adequate.

In spite of its novelty, the dialectical approach is essentially a metaphysical one, since its logic is not merely the formal science of implication without existential import, but the super-science of the ultimate nature off Reality.

It would he unfair and incorrect to say that Hegel lacked a meta-philosophy. But his meta-philosophy was inadequate. His approach lacked the precision of Kant, and was not rooted in a neutral and critical analysis of the types and functions of language. He was thus prompted to equate a partly persuasive definitional system with a descriptive super-science, possessing universal and eternal truth. The partly conventional component of his dialectical logic and the possibility of alternative concrete interpretations of his sets of dialectical triads was not envisioned by him. Apart from this serious methodological confusion, his concrete dialectical analyses of several concepts appear to be Procrustean attempts forcefully to fit the fact into the triad.

However, the sweep and depth of his knowledge of history and the social and cultural sciences of his time was the greatest single factor in the emergence of, what I have termed as, the cultural approach to philosophy.

Conclusion

Metaphysics as a super-science is impossible. The illusion of its methodological validity is the product of a pre-critical or pre-analytical approach. The metaphysical analysis, which is practised by speculative philosophers, does not question the hidden assumptions of the metaphysical conceptual field. However, a scientific onto-cosmology attempted by Whitehead, as an abstract conceptual scheme to unify and locate empirical data and procedures, or Ontology, in the sense of a rigorous and systematic analysis of basic concepts, and their integration into a multi-layered conceptual system, as attempted by Hartmann are possible. But this conception is radically different from the traditional conception of metaphysics as a super-science.

Chapter 4

The Cultural Approach to Philosophy

General Introduction

The cultural approach does not repudiate metaphysics as such, though it rejects metaphysics as a super-science or transcendental ontology. The cultural approach transforms Metaphysics from an *Ontology* into a *Weltanschauung* or world view. It advances a meta-philosophical conception of the nature, function and methodology of philosophical theories. It holds that traditional philosophy had misconceived the nature and function of metaphysics and confused philosophical interpretation with scientific explanation. Metaphysics was not concerned with trans empirical facts, as distinguished from empirical facts, studied by Physics or other natural sciences.

It was concerned with modes or patterns of organizing the totality of human experience into a meaningful whole. It functioned in a different dimension altogether as art does from technology. But just as art cannot function without techniques, metaphysics cannot function in isolation from factual knowledge. Neither is it just like poetry or religion. It is *sui generis*. The nature and function of metaphysical statements must be carefully explored. Traditional metaphysicians assimilated them to factual statements about *Ultimate Reality*. The *Logical Positivists* took these pretensions literally and seriously, and prescribed tests of meaningfulness and truth, that were imported from the sphere of factual discourse. It is not surprising that metaphysical statements fared badly and were branded as nonsense. The cultural approach tries to understand the nature of metaphysics, not at its face value, but through a study of its function in human life, and through viewing metaphysics as organically related to the concrete social and cultural matrix of man. The cultural approach crystallized in Germany in the 19th century as a result of the blooming of the social and cultural sciences. Two basic concepts were crucial in suggesting this approach. One was the concept of society or a social group as an organic developing totality with a life history. This may be called the concept of *social organism* or *societal personality.* The other was the concept of cultural *gestalt* or configuration; Hegel's was the most important single influence in the formation of these concepts.

The first concept, if literally understood, is obviously misleading. But, understood in the functional sense, it is highly illuminating, since it draws our attention to important observable social facts, and the tremendous dependence of the individual upon the social group in which he is born and brought up. He may not be a cell of an organism. He may even be said to have an independent existence, in a sense in which the group does not exist independently of, and over and above, the individuals. Yet, as far as the concrete and distinctively human content of his life is concerned-namely the manifold of thinking, feeling and willing-this is fashioned and molded by his situational matrix. In this sense the individual is dependent upon his group, and is a cell in the organism.

Now the concept of the societal organism, once it was sufficiently crystallized, inevitably led to the systematic study of different societal units in their structural and functional aspects. Thus, Sociology and later on Sociography and Cultural Anthropology were born.

Secondly, the concept of cultural *gestalt* directed the social scientist to discover and identify the underlying structure or *gestalt* of the concrete cultural responses of a societal unit. The assumption was that the various responses in the fields of morality, religion, art, philosophy,

The Cultural Approach to Philosophy

science, politics, etcetera were not disconnected with each other, but that they exhibited a *determinate pattern* or *gestalt*. This was termed the *spirit* of the culture of a group, it should, however, not be confused with the *Absolute Spirit* of Hegel.

The concept of cultural *gestalt* implied that the philosophy of a group was interlinked with the rest of its cultural content, and that it could not be understood in isolation. It molded and influenced and was in turn, itself influenced, by the concrete cultural and situational matrix of the individual. Hegel, thus, initiated the approach that developed into the historical or sociological materialism of Karl Marx and the *Lebensphilosophie* of Dilthey, Troeltsch, Eucken and others. The movement of *Historicism* is only a version of *Lebensphilosophie* in the wider sense.

Marx's thought acquired a distinct shade obviously because of his practical concern with the problem of changing *Reality* instead of merely understanding it. The cognate concepts of (a) ideology as a super-structure built or evolved by the thinkers of a group to protect and stabilize its existing power and economic structure, and (b) the situational determination of thought dominate the philosophical content and approach of Marx to a much more pronounced degree than in the case of Dewey or Dilthey. They make him eloquently polemical instead of calmly analytical. He does not concern himself with a detailed delineation of the different world views or value systems in the manner of Dilthey and Scheler. Moreover, he does not adopt a spectators attitude towards these world views, but the attitude of a participant. Dilthey posited a recurring tendency of the main world views, *Materialism* or *Naturalism, Idealism* or *Theism*, and *Positivism* to recur in human history. But Marx posited a single track that led towards the withering away of rival philosophies together with class conflict and the nation states.

The approach of *Lebenephilosophie* finds a distinct echo in the thought of John Dewey, who repeatedly stressed the need to understand that the problems of philosophers were theoretical and abstract, and hence, misleading versions of the problems of men at a particular stage of human history. Instead of solving the problems of philosophers in an isolated and abstract speculative or intellectual manner, they should first be correlated with the historical situation of men. This alone would lead to their proper formulation, and to a grasp of their genuine nature, and the social significance or the concrete consequences of the alternative answers. The answers, Dewey further held, were to be tested and accepted on the basis of their usefulness to human values. By raising the question of the criterion of validity, Dewey went further than Dilthey, who was content to analyze and classify the various world views as integral elements of a cultural gestalt, and to correlate them with different situational matrices.

The conceptual field of a philosopher is constituted by his foundational assumptions. These assumptions are given a *push* in a direction, which is determined partly by the nature of the assumptions themselves, and partly by the *leitmotif* of the philosopher. This *leitmotif* is largely a cultural phenomenon, that is, the product of cultural conditioning. But it is not entirely uniform among the philosophers of a group. It has its own subtle nuances in different individual philosophers. It is these nuances that are the part causes of the concrete differences that arise within the context of an overall agreement or a common world view.

The conceptual field or foundational assumptions of the cultural approach to philosophy are as follows: (a) Mans dependence upon society in the form of cultural conditioning, (b) Cultural responses form a gestalt, (c) Philosophy as an abstract conceptual response is organically related to other responses like art, morality, religion etcetera. (d) Philosophical world views are neither true nor false, but valid or invalid, (e) Philosophical world views must, therefore, be grasped and enjoyed like art forms rather than proved or disproved like logico-mathematical statements and hypotheses.

Within this broad conceptual field, the following questions and tasks arise: What are the concrete features of the various patterns of

The Cultural Approach to Philosophy

world views? What are their basic types? What is the exact role of the various features of the situational matrix in the molding of world views? What is the value system implicit in different world views? How do world views change? In what sense are world views true or false and what are the criteria of their truth? What are the concrete similarities and differences between world views on the one hand, and science, poetry, religion, etcetera on the other? Some of these questions will be considered in this chapter.

Delineation of the Cultural Approach

Culture may be defined as an evaluatively guided modification of a pre-existing natural state of affairs. Thus, leveling, ploughing the earth and growing crops are culture of the earth or agriculture. Exercising the body to develop it is culture of the body or physical culture. Training a child not to cry when he cannot spot his mother working in the kitchen is culture of the feelings or emotions. Exhorting a child that it is wrong to tell lies, or grab his little sisters toys, is the culture of evaluation and attitudes, or moral culture. Similarly, there is the culture of reasoning or inference (logical training), the culture of taste (aesthetic training), etcetera. Cultural training in the widest sense begins at the birth of an individual in a group. The learning process modifies the natural states of affairs, that is, the attitudes the child would have developed if left in a state of nature. The learning process covers the language, gestures, customs, habits, attitudes towards the in-group and out-group, aesthetic taste, the value scale and religious beliefs etcetera. But what is of crucial importance from the viewpoint of philosophy is the assimilation by the growing youth of the conceptual field current in the group. The concept of a conceptual field or frame supplies the key to the cultural approach to philosophy. A pre-critical world view is primarily a more or less systematic and developed form of the conceptual field current in the group.

It is illuminating to say that philosophy is the culture of conceptual fields or world views, natural science is the culture of perceptual fields and judgments, morality is the culture of evaluations and volitions, art is the culture of taste, while religion, in the traditional sense, is the commitment to a particular world view, inspired by faith.

Man is never satisfied with bare description. He always tries to fit his perceptual experience of particulars into unifying conceptual frames or systems. An accurate description of, say an egg, is only a part of the knowledge about the egg. Unless the observer knows the relation of an egg to a living organism etcetera, the bare physical description, however accurate and complete, of the egg, neither exhausts the knowledge about the egg, nor satisfies the human urge towards order and system in the elements of his experience. Perception starts, as it were, a circuit that is closed only by *conceptual unification.*

This conceptual unification is of two distinct kinds, and within each kind, there is a further distinction of levels or of range. It is of crucial importance not to mix up these two kinds of unification. The first type is descriptive, while the second is interpretative. A scientific unification is essentially descriptive and predictive. Prediction, however, is nothing but fore-description. Hence, it is verifiable. The second type is interpretative.

Interpretation, as understood here, is not pseudo-description or pseudo-explanation. It is a distinct activity, just as the activity of evaluation is distinct from that of description. Philosophical interpretation is an activity that may he called *existential unification* or *existential analogizing.* The individual attempts to unify the foundational features of human experience of the world, not in order to predict (as is the purpose of science), nor in order to give aesthetic joy to him self or others (as is the purpose of fine arts or poetry), but in order to relate himself in a total manner to the universe. This no doubt provides the individual with aesthetic satisfaction. But the *leitmotif* or spirit behind this attempt is radically different. Such an *existential unification* both leads to and is demanded by a deep yearning in man to commit himself to a total world view, inclusive of a value system. This *existential unification* provides something far deeper and much more significant than the aesthetic joy provided by poetry. It leads to basic ethical choices. The route from a world view to a value system is as significant as the route from a value system to a world view.

This basic kind of unification has been termed existential, to show its central significance and importance in the economy of the individuals existence. The term *existential unification* was suggested by the existential choice referred to by contemporary Existentialists. This *existential unification* is achieved through analogical thinking that is, viewing the universe as a whole in terms of an analogy with a key or basic feature of human experience. Different philosophers are liable to be gripped or struck by different features.

Features of human experience may be correlated with the time honored and reputable division of experience into knowing, feeling and willing. Thus, regular sequence in the perceptual experience of man is a feature of the knowing process, on the one hand, and of the world on the other. The feature of unity in variety and variety in unity, in the sense of the existence of numerous particulars or individuals of a common species or type, is another such feature. The contrast between appearance and reality, form and matter, and the reversible transformation of one state or condition of matter into another, are other striking examples. Other features of human experience, for example, purpose, striving, sense of power as well as of helplessness, aesthetic and ethical evaluation, optimism and despair etcetera are correlated with feeling or willing.

Different philosophers gravitate towards some favored feature of human experience and make it the foundation for the activity of *existential unification*. Since such unification is analogical, it would perhaps be illuminating to call it existential analogizing. This brings out its metaphysical component and affinity with poetry, and yet keeps it distinct. An *existential unification* is neither a pseudo-hypothesis or pre-scientific explanation, nor a poetic analogy. It is *sui generis*. Its assimilation to either one type of discourse or the other is a grave methodological error, which has been perpetrated in the past by a lack of a critical meta-philosophy. An *existential unification* both resembles and differs from the scientific and poetic types of discourse.

The confusion of *existential unifications* or, in plain terms, philosophical world views with hypotheses, naturally leads to a crucial objection against metaphysical statements, namely, their un-verifiability. They are, then liable to be dismissed as non-sense, or as pseudo-hypotheses of the pre-scientific age. The confusion of philosophical world views with poetry, on the other hand, does not lead to their unceremonious dismissal. But it excessively demotes the status of philosophical world views. They are stripped of their truth claims or ontological pretensions and given the same status and privileges as poetry. It is believed that this status is high enough and ought to keep philosophy satisfied. But this state of affairs certainly discourages the quest for the analysis and construction of world views. The deeper significance of an *existential unification* is missed by this view.

To conclude this section, the urge for *conceptual unification* of an existential type, that is, the urge for philosophical interpretation of the basic features of human experience is an identifiable and distinct urge. It has been and probably will remain operative in all men, explicitly or implicitly.

Consider some examples from the theistic conceptual field or world view. The sight of human suffering prompts the theist to interpret it, or locate it in a conceptual field, whether as a penalty for sins, or a test of faith, or a means of inner development etcetera. Similarly, a particular judgment, or action, for example, '*God punished Tom*', or '*Tom gave charity to please God*', becomes meaningful only when Tom antecedently accepts the corresponding frame of reference; the theological. This field is the fixed frame of reference into which all sets of experiences are located, even as iron filings fall into a pattern around a magnet. The mass of data which otherwise would have been inchoate spatio-temporal slices are cultured, or patterned. Consider two persons watching the same game of cricket. One is an expert, while the other knows next to nothing about it. The spatio-temporal slices constituting the game are common to both observers. But for the expert, there is a frame of reference; the rules of the game, the arrangement of the field, etcetera, into which those slices are fitted. For the other lacking in a frame of reference, the slices are like a foreign language that is a series of sounds, but without sense.

Consider: *'Poverty is a Divine Scheme for developing the latent powers in man'.* This is a theological conceptual field for locating the fact that sometimes poverty does develop the latent power of individuals. The fact is the empirical manifold, intertwined with the interpretive manifold.

The full conceptual field may be described as follows: *'God has created the universe and rules and governs it to the last detail. All states of affairs fulfill the Plan. Poverty fulfils His purpose of developing the latent powers of men, and qualifying them for the kingdom of Heaven. God is cruel to be kind to His creation'.*

An alternative conceptual field for locating the fact of poverty, which exists in the world, is in the psychological field. *'Poverty acts as a challenge and stimulus to work hard. It has not been produced by God to test men or improve their character. It exists due to specifiable causes. Analogically, cold does not exist so that men may put on overcoats and light fires. Rather cold acts as a challenge to man who responds in this way. Events occur according to descriptive laws and not according to prescriptive commands of a Divine Being'.*

The acceptance or rejection of a particular conceptual field for one set of facts leads to corresponding or cognate fields for other sets of facts or experiences. The individual accepting the scientific-psychological field to locate social facts like poverty etcetera would tend to accept the scientific physico-chemical frame to locate natural facts like an earthquake etcetera. The individual accepting the theological field would tend to locate in it both social and natural facts. To refute an explanation or interpretation without examining the field is methodologically wrong.

One may accept a basic conceptual field, but differ within that field. This suggests the concept of conceptual figure within a field. It may be a statement, a hypothesis or an interpretation. For example, the interpretation that pain and evil are Divine means for the production of good, and the interpretation that pain and evil are Divine tests of human character, are two different conceptual figures within the same field. Similarly, *Ontological Materialism* or *Idealism* are two contradictory conceptual figures in the field of metaphysics as a super-science describing *Reality*.

Metaphysical systems are prima facie cognitive, descriptive of *Ultimate Reality* and logically deduced, having nothing to do with the attitudes and values of the individual. But the cultural approach, in agreement with the current ordinary language approach, and the once powerful logical positivist approach, rejects these prima facie claims. This, however, does not mean that its meta-philosophical foundation is the same as theirs. It rejects these claims for different reasons.

A philosophical world view emerges from the pre-philosophical group conceptual field, which predisposes the philosopher towards a particular conceptual direction. But all philosophers do not start in a uniform relationship with their inherited conceptual field. Some philosophers merely articulate, systematize and clarify the groups implicit world view, removing contradictions that may be latent in its crude popular expression. Other philosophers reconstruct the pattern to a greater or less extent. They not only represent the culture of which they are a product, but are also its constructive critics. They thus help the process of conceptual evolution in the matrix of historical change.

The functions of representation and criticism are present in varying proportions in all philosophers. When the representative function preponderates, we have a traditional conservative philosopher. When it is the other way round; we have a radical philosopher who is a critic of his age. As an extreme case, we have a conceptual rebel.

World views are both the products of the age as well as periodically recurring types. But every age and society fills the frame with its own distinctive details. The general or generic conceptual frame may also undergo considerable structural change without, however, losing its identity or the core of its approach. Every age has its style of conceptual architecture. One must, therefore, not take others or even him self too seriously as the abiding model. Possibly those philosophers who had anticipated their becoming out of date and outmoded, will be remembered with greater respect than will be others.

The Changing Patterns of World Views

Why do conceptual fields change and why do they differ in the first instance. Only an indication of the general approach can be given here. Thinking always takes place in a conceptual frame. Philosophy comes much later. It is born from the womb of current cultural frames, or conceptual fields after a great deal of refinement of language and of the conceptual apparatus has taken place.

Due to the wide variety of the natural environment of human societies as well as the subtle differences in the concrete personality structure of human beings (no matter due to what factors), a variety of conceptual fields emerge in different societies. When they are elaborated conceptually in the form of philosophical world views or systems, the diversity persists and is further crystallized. These systems then serve to reinforce and perpetuate the original conceptual frames by giving them the aura of certainty, objective truth and finality. Members of the group tend to become all the more ethnocentric and fixed in these world views. The quarrels and the disputes of the philosophers of the groups become family quarrels that lie within the frame, and are not about the frame. However, there may be a few notable exceptions.

Different cultural patterns arise in different societies and ages due to the interaction of a number of factors; physical, climatic, psychological etcetera. The process of cultural differentiation from a parent pattern, as in the case of language, may partly account for those differences.

But this explanation leaves out the original differences that might have and probably did exist between the diverse cultural patterns.

To a certain extent these differences can be correlated with external factors. To the extent that this is possible, this correlation should be attempted. For example, the custom of meat eating can be correlated with cold regions where agriculture or horticulture is not easily possible. The attitudes of people in an isolated island or mountainous corner would differ from the desert Bedouin or the sea-faring Phoenicians, etcetera. But beyond these limits, we are forced to say that the original differences, if any, in the cultural patterns are the ultimate data of sociological science.

A comparison with biological or organic evolution would be useful in this context. According to Darwin, the various organisms have evolved due to the operation of natural selection upon minute variations in the cells of organisms over very long periods. These variations are accepted as an ultimate brute fact. The law '*like produces like but not just like*', is not an explanation, but rather an admission of ultimacy. Similarly, we may say that the differences in human responses are due partly to identifiable factors, and partly to their being uniquely individual, even though similar.

Conceptual fields, however, change in a changing universe. The advance of factual knowledge demands fresh, more complex and comprehensive conceptual fields to locate fields. Moreover, inter group contacts taking place due to conquests, trade, and travel etcetera, result in the confrontation of diverse conceptual frames, or judgments arising there from, in the mind of individuals. This contact is extremely fertile for change. But the personality traits of the individual as well as his concrete life situation partly determine the extent and depth of change in the conceptual field. There are several patterns of individual adaptation.

The epistemo-dynamics of conceptual fields enables us to see how the various conceptual fields and interpretations arise naturally in the total situational or life field. For example, the anthropomorphic theological field comes naturally to man in the pre-technological situation. This field takes a long time to develop from a crude animism, via Polytheism etcetera. The situational changes like the invention of agriculture, the mingling of various cultures in war and peace, the changing patterns of social relationships and power distribution etcetera are all contributory factors in the formation or evocation of conceptual fields. Had we moderns been placed in past situations, we too would have responded in a similar conceptual fashion, just as centuries ago we would have lived in mud houses, and not skyscrapers. However, the creative thinkers of the group go beyond the current conceptual structures, and gradually carry others with them. This constitutes conceptual evolution.

World Views and Truth

If philosophical theories and systems are conceptual patterns, then how and in what sense can they be true or false? A landscape or a musical composition may be good or bad. But there is no sense in judging them to be true or false. If, however, philosophy claims to be a conceptual picture of the universe, as a portrait is of an individual, say, Napoleon, then the terms true or false are applicable to philosophy. But in the case of a portrait, we have the original subject as well as the painting, and the two can be compared. Now where is the original subject in the case of the universe? Surely, the observed features of the universe are there. But a philosophical theory is not descriptive.

Consider the case of a number of architects, each pressing his design for acceptance by the town planners. There is no standard or Platonic design, with reference to which the claims of the architects could be tested and settled. Even if there were such design, but was in principle inaccessible, there would be no point in claiming truth for a particular design. All that legitimately could be claimed by an architect was that his particular design had such and such advantages under specified conditions, apart from aesthetic value.

Philosophers who construct conceptual systems claiming them to he true, are not like these architects. There is no standard conceptual model to serve as a criterion of the truth or falsity of the conceptual schemes offered. To give another illustration, the crude stone implements or tools and huts of our ancestor were not *false* even as our electronic hands and needles and multi-storied buildings are not *true*. All we can say is that a primitive hut is far less useful (though not useless) and hence unacceptable to modern man.

It might be objected that some scientific theories too cannot be thus compared with an original model, and are yet judged as true or false. But in such cases the deductive consequences of those scientific hypotheses are always verifiable (in theory, if not in practice due to some practical impediment which is in principle removable). Unfortunately metaphysical theories like Plato's *Theory of Ideas* or Spinoza's *Theory of Substance* have no verifiable consequences.

To ask whether world views are objectively true or not is, thus, to raise an improper question. The question of the truth of world views arises because the word *true* is used in many different senses and contexts. We are liable to raise questions concerning truth, which though quite proper in one context, are quite improper in others. To ask whether the truth of an attitude, a philosophy, religion or art is objective or subjective is to assimilate the use of *true* in these contexts to the use of *true* in descriptive contexts. And just as descriptive statements cannot be both true and false, but must be either true or false, similarly (it is thought) some one particular world view must be true and all others false. Again, just as the *true descriptive statement is objectively true*, describes the nature of the real object, similarly (it is thought) the true world view describes the nature of the real universe as a whole. The true world view is objective and mirrors the intrinsic nature of Reality without any distortion or refraction. All other views are distorted, hence subjective

The entire problem of objectivity/subjectivity of world views arises because of the assimilation of the truth of world views to the *truth* of descriptive and logico-mathematical statements due to the prior assimilation of world views or conceptual fields to descriptive statements

The Cultural Approach to Philosophy

and scientific hypotheses. Ethical statements, or world views can be true, or false, objective or subjective no less than descriptive statements. But the sense of *true* or *false*, or the use of these words differs in each case. The failure to identify the different uses in different contexts of the same word *true* or *false* generates the problem. Before analyzing, the exact sense of *true* in the, context of world views together with the criteria, of their *truth,* it is important to consider the relationship, if any, between world views and value systems.

A close examination of world views suggests that their pattern and structure correspond with value systems tacitly or implicitly held. If, for example, inner freedom is held as a higher value than group solidarity or discipline, then, it appears to me that Pantheism, or immanent theism, rather than the transcendental version of theism would appeal to the religious thinker.

The realization that philosophical systems are ultimately rooted in a covert value system prevents the meta-philosopher from attacking or defending those philosophical systems on the linguistic or logical plane in isolation from their corresponding value systems. It is important to focus attention upon the source and function of philosophical theories.

The full import of a philosophical system will elude us unless we can identify the value system from which it has sprung and evolved with the help of logical systematization. Once this is done, we grasp the *raison d'etere* of the philosophical system. This approach is analogous to the discovery of the linguistic sources of the inclination to make statement S1 or S2 or S3. The importance of the discovery of the sources of philosophical perplexity has been convincingly shown by Wittgenstein, Wisdom, Ryle, and many other contemporary philosophers of the ordinary language school. But the sources are not merely linguistic.

The mere identification by a person of the value system behind a philosophical theory he accepts, may lead to some significant modification in the theory. Just as self-analysis, or Psychoanalysis may lead to the weakening or even disappearance of an attitude, without any moral exhortation, similarly philosophical theories may be out-grown or transcended without intellectual refutation, that is, without going into the question of their truth or falsity as such. When the hidden value system is brought to the surface, congealed conceptual patterns or theories may, and, at times, do dissolve as does wax before fire. The reason is that the individual grasps more or less clearly the source of the inclination towards a particular formulation or view. This, however, does not render conceptual or linguistic analysis of those views methodologically superfluous.

The Criteria of Validity of World Views

If the use of the concepts *true* or *false, objectively true* or *subjectively true* in the context of philosophical systems and theories differs from their use in the context of verifiable descriptive statements, does this land us in the night where all cats are black? Do we step into the bog of arbitrariness with no solid ground of rational conviction? No. All that is required is the substitution of the concept of methodological validity in the place of truth. The criteria of validity of word views can only be recommendatory norms for regulating their acceptance or rejection. The criteria can only be postulated, but not proved. In this respect they are similar to the requirements of scientific method. Empirical statements or hypotheses are proved or established on the basis of the scientific method. But the scientific method itself cannot be proved or established as true, apart from being shown as actually fruitful or useful. The validity of the scientific method cannot be demonstrated to a person who rejects it. But he can rightly be asked to put forward his alternative method. There must be some criteria of truth and some method or agreed procedure for the acceptance or rejection of truth claims. Otherwise there would be complete confusion and despair. This would tend to extinguish the human search for truth and mutual agreement. A minimum measure of agreement is the foundation of joint living.

I do not propose to give here a detailed exposition of the criteria of validity, or the requirements of the interpretative method, as it may aptly be called. Broadly speaking, they are the same as in the case of the scientific method, namely, simplicity, comprehensiveness, consistency, and pragmatic fruitfulness, but without the important requirement of verifiability.

Verifiability in the scientific sense cannot have any applicability to world views, if we antecedently exclude them from the domain of true or false as used in descriptive contexts. If world views are admittedly not descriptive of a trans-empirical *Ultimate Reality*, that is, if world views are not the statements belonging to a super-science, but are modes of *conceptual unification* of the foundational features of human experience, then the pertinent question is not of their verification, but rather of the identification of the key category or *categorical analogy* used for the purpose of unification.

A world view as a *conceptual unification* grows out of the inclination to assimilate the foundational features of human experience to some one favored model or feature of experience. This assimilation is effected through a kind of analogical thinking, which bears a resemblance to both poetry and factual discourse, without being reducible to either. The clarification of the detailed logic of the language of world views is a most vital philosophical task. But it cannot be attempted in this essay. I can only throw a hint that just as many ethical statements are neither purely evaluative, nor purely descriptive, similarly statements expressing world views are neither purely analogical or poetic, nor purely factual. They have both components. Hence, though they are not verifiable, they may be more or less applicable to human experience. It is very difficult to clarify this suggested term. But the nearest example I can think of is the aptness of a metaphor or simile. What makes a metaphor *apt* is different to pinpoint. Yet aptness is not arbitrary.

The *applicability* of a world view can be established rationally, albeit to a limited point, as in the case of concrete ethical reasoning. In so far as the consequences of actions are at least partly verifiable, empirical considerations are relevant to ethical reasoning. Similarly, up to a point, empirical considerations, or the observed features of the universe, like law and order, utility etcetera, prima facie may support or lead to a world view. But beyond that point, empirical considerations cease to be relevant. The facts may be agreed upon and yet may be interpreted quite differently. No world view logically or deductively implies facts that could be verified and thereby constitute a proof of its truth. If this were the case, philosophical controversy would have ceased. Thus there is no conclusive test of the *applicability* of a world view.

Conclusion

An uncritically accepted world view is a simple function of cultural conditioning. Even the deliberate choice of the key model is partly a function of the personality structure and value system of the individual. The concrete dynamics of the impact of the value system upon the world view is a very important field of enquiry.

Although the formulation and application of the criteria of validity of world views is essential, and also partly fruitful for forging agreement, no recommended criteria can totally eliminate disagreement and the conflict of world views. If value systems can never be inductively or deductively established, then world views, which are rooted in those value systems, also cannot be so established. A deep and ineradicable sense of logical uncertainty, if not of philosophical perplexity, appears to be the inevitable destiny of man.

CHAPTER 5

THE ANALYTICAL APPROACH TO PHILOSOPHY

GENERAL INTRODUCTION

The progressive encroachment by science upon the traditional domain of philosophy in the 19th century unavoidably forced the attention of philosophers upon meta-philosophical issues. The striking feature of the situation, however, was the growing agreement between different scientists in the midst of a chronic controversy among philosophers. Acute philosophers say, Spinoza and Leibniz, held mutually contradictory theories like Monism and Monadism to be either self-evident or deductively certain. The disagreements of scientists, on the other hand, were not so sharp, to begin with; in any case they were being progressively reduced. Advances in mathematics and symbolic logic, and the strict requirements of the scientific method; verifiability and explanatory fruitfulness of hypotheses; all led to a rigorous analysis of scientific concepts. Many current and even respectable concepts of science were found to be lacking in the above qualities. Thus, *ether, simultaneity,* and *absolute motion* etcetera, had either to be dropped or reconstructed to become reputable. This clarificatory activity, once started in the sphere of science and mathematics, was inevitably extended to the sphere of philosophy. Thus, the 19th century situation of Europe and America evoked the analytical approach in the widest sense of the term. The *leitmotif* of the analytical approach to philosophy is to diagnose and cure philosophical disagreement. This movement has reached its peak in our own times.

Five Approaches To Philosophy

The *Positivism* of Comte and Mach was the earliest version of the 19th century analytical approach. Positivism holds mathematical and scientific knowledge as the Paradigm case of knowledge, and judges all other cases by the criteria of validity contained in the scientific method. A pure analytical approach, ideally speaking, should be neutral, and not start with such a predilection toward a favored type of discourse. Positivism is thus, strictly speaking, a distinct approach. Since, however, it functionally leads to analysis as the only activity of philosophy, it is reasonable to regard it as one of the species of the analytical approach in the wider sense. The *Pragmaticism* of C.S. Pierce, and the Pragmatism of William James and Dewey were cognate approaches, evoked by the same situation. The title of Pierces famous essay, *How To Make Our Ideas Clear,* reflects the basic orientation and *leitmotif* of his thinking. A.B. Johnson was another pioneer of the analytical approach. But his recognition has come only in our own time. The Phenomenology of Edmund Husserl was likewise analytical, though in a completely different setting. Pragmatism may thus be regarded as the American version of the analytical approach, while Phenomenology the German version.

The analytical approach to philosophy is not and cannot be an entirely new approach, for the simple reason that analysis, in some form or the other, is inseparable from systematic thinking. The most speculative or metaphysical philosopher has to analyze the statements of others and his own for the purposes of exposition and criticism, if not clarification for its own sake. When, however, clarificatory activity predominates over the attempt to construct a comprehensive world view or ontological system etcetera, or when the latter activity is deliberately avoided, whether temporarily or permanently, the approach may rightly be termed analytical. Even in this sense, there can be no rigid separation between analytical and speculative philosophers. Plato, Aristotle, Spinoza, Berkeley, Leibniz, Kant, Bradley and James are both analytical and speculative in different phases or portions of their works. Passages in Plato's *Theatetus* or *Philebus* could well be attributed to a contemporary analytical philosopher. Berkeley's charge that philosophers believing in material substance use an empty word is strikingly similar to the charge made by *Logical Positivists* and others against metaphysical concepts and statements. Hume's assessment of metaphysical reasoning as nothing but sophistry and illusion is also well known. The analysis of statements into analytic and synthetic etcetera, by Kant and Leibniz, and Kant's conception of the status and genesis of metaphysics is the product of an analytical approach to philosophy.

What then is the justification of positing a distinct analytical approach to philosophy? The justification lies in the explicit and deliberate restriction to analysis by many modern philosophers on the assumption that speculation is methodologically improper, since unverifiable, or its real nature and function, as distinguished from its prima facie nature, render speculation useless. Or the assumption may be that speculation is useless unless preceded by rigorous and sustained analysis covering a very wide area of thought, which condition will long remain unfulfilled. The modern approach, functionally speaking, equates philosophy with clarification of concepts and statements. In some cases it reduces philosophy to analysis without any remainder.

The analytical approach is not single and uniform. It has several species or varieties, and objections against one variety cannot be applied ipso facto against others. We shall consider the philosophical analysis of Moore and Russell, the logical positivistic analysis of the Vienna Circle, the linguistic analysis of contemporary philosophers, and also the phenomenological analysis of Husserl.

THE PHILOSOPHICAL ANALYSIS OF MOORE AND RUSSELL

Moore and Russell were the principal architects of the analytical approach to philosophy in Britain. Together they broke the spell of Bradley and Neo-Hegelianism; Moore with the help of his intellectual honesty and penetrative simplicity, Russell with the weapons of logic and Mathematics. Close as their collaboration was in the practice of philosophy, they differed in their theoretical approach in important respects. Hence it would be desirable to consider their meta-philosophy separately.

(I) MOORE

Moore, like Russell started as a follower and admirer of Bradley. But the notorious disagreements between philosophers as well as the disagreement between their theory and practice prompted him to question the doing of philosophy in the grand speculative manner. He was struck by the fact that philosophers asserted statements that were at variance with common sense beliefs, and that this discrepancy did not at all bother the philosophers as if it were a matter of no significance or consequence. But while philosophers might have thus lightly repudiated common sense beliefs, they nevertheless acted as if they were true. One is here apt to be reminded of the candid confessions of Hume in the *Treatise*, about his doubts and questioning disappearing when he left the philosophers desk and returned to the daily tasks and activities of normal living. Moore was too honest and earnest to ignore this fact. For him philosophy was not a mere intellectual game for displaying his intellectual brilliance and subtlety at the expense of common sense beliefs and convictions. For him philosophy was the honest pursuit of truth and consistency in both thought and action.

Moore felt that he, for his part, could not brush aside so lightly a number of basic common sense beliefs and convictions, such as, I have a body; I was born a certain number of years ago; there are physical objects and other persons outside me etcetera. He could not help thinking that these beliefs were almost certainly true. If so, he could not legitimately assert other philosophical statements that were incompatible with these basic beliefs. Moore enumerated these in his famous paper; *A Defense of Common Sense*. They were not merely respectable enough to be defended by philosophers, but were most certainly true, and thus did not stand in any need of defense. This led to a transformation of the philosophical enterprise as hitherto practiced. This candid and, in a sense, revolutionary acceptance by Moore of the truth of common sense beliefs, did not mean that he was not puzzled about them, or that these beliefs did pose any problems for him. Had this been case, philosophy, would have become superfluous. Moore emphasized that while he was certain of the truth of these basic beliefs, he was not at all clear about their meaning or analysis. To analyze them was precisely the task of philosophy.

What did Moore mean by analysis? Moore never went explicitly into meta-philosophical or methodological questions. He preferred to practice analysis rather than propound a theory of analysis. But what he actually did was to attempt a logical translation of the statement that was being analyzed. The analysis or the *analysiens*, must be clearer and simpler than the *analysandum* or the expression sought to be analyzed, yet both must be exactly equivalent in meaning. To analyze was, thus, to reduce a statement to an equivalent but simpler statement or a set of such statements. A simple statement was one which was further irreducible and whose meaning could be grasped only ostensively. Thus, *'this is a hand'* was not simple, since it could be reduced to statements about sense data, such as, *'I see such and such a patch of such and such a color'*.

Now Moore's trouble was that no attempted analysis satisfied the stringent conditions of simplicity and equivalence that he had prescribed to himself. Both perceptual and ethical statements could not be analyzed without remainder. Thus, Moore was never happy with, say, a phenomenalistic analysis of physical object statements. Nor was he happy with any form of a naturalistic analysis of ethical statements. Moore was thus compelled to say that *good* was an unanalyzable simple property, just like yellow. He was likewise led to admit that no proffered analysis of physical object statements was satisfactory, since the exact relationship between sense data and the physical object had not been ascertained. This amounted to saying that the term *physical object* though not simple, was also unanalyzable, like the term *good*.

How and why was Moore led to lay special emphasis upon analysis? He himself alludes to his inability to understand the exact meaning or sense of propositions such as, *Time is unreal* or *Reality is spiritual* etcetera, made by philosophers. It was net, that he could not significantly or correctly employ such statements, or that he was unfamiliar with the English language in which they were made. As a matter of fact, at one time, he himself employed similar statements while arguing about the ultimate nature of *Reality* etcetera. But he later on realized that his understanding of such statements was very inadequate and nebulous.

Secondly, Moore realized that words were ambiguous. Thus, the word *real* could be applied to a number of objects. We speak of *real love, real loss, a real beard,* or *pistol, real gold,* and *real existence* etcetera. Now what exactly was signified by the adjective real in the above different usages was an important question. But it could not be, answered offhand without a very careful and laborious analysis of the exact meaning of the word *real*.

Thirdly, it was clearly unprofitable and improper to answer philosophical questions unless the exact meaning of a question had been ascertained. Often different questions were posed behind a common verbal formulation. For example, the question, '*What is good?*', could mean two different things. It might be a question about the meaning of the term *good*, or it might be a question about the things that are good. Moore made a clear distinction between these two tasks, and held that a good deal of ethical, disagreement and controversy was due to confusing these two distinct questions.

Fourthly, a lull grasp of the logic of philosophical statements, that is, (a) the regressive conditions required for their truth, together with their deductive implications, and (b) an over-all view of the mutual compatibility or incompatibility of philosophical theories, and other beliefs that were prima facie true, was a necessary precondition of the critical acceptance or rejection of philosophical views. Unfortunately many philosophers were in a hurry to prove or disprove statements. They thought they had established that *Time is Unreal*, or *Matter does not exist independently of Mind*, or *Reality is spiritual* when only part of the necessary conditions had been fulfilled. In such cases the grounds given were not adequate for the conclusion, even though the conclusion might be true.

Analysis was thus essential for breaking through the confusions, obscurities, chronic controversies, interminable and inconclusive debates and paradoxical conclusions that were the deposit of the philosophical enterprise as hitherto conducted. An effective restraint upon speculation and concentration upon the modest but foundational task of clarification of the meanings and mutual interrelations of statements was vital for genuine philosophical progress, according to Moore. But he never questioned, at least theoretically, the traditional aim of philosophy, namely study of the ultimate *nature* of *Reality* as a whole. Analysis was the tool par excellence of the philosopher and a means to the settlement of philosophical disputes.

Limitations of Moore's Approach

Moore clearly and sharply draws our attention to the phenomenon of philosophical paradox and disagreement. But he does not diagnose it fully. Hastiness, confusion and fallacious reasoning are adjudged as the causes of odd views and paradoxes. But this does not touch the root of the matter, although correct as far as it goes.

Moore's conception of analysis and clarification is restricted to the meaning of statements, and does not embrace the identification and description of the functions or uses of words, in the logical, as distinguished from their grammatical sense. The full limitations of Moore's analysis are brought out in the section on linguistic analysis. However, they do not reduce the crucial role of Moore in the metamorphosis of 20th century philosophy.

(II) Russell

Russell's approach of *Logical Atomism* is an avowedly metaphysical approach, much more so than the philosophical analytical approach of Moore. Yet Russell's approach must be classified as analytical, since he holds logical analysis to be the foundation and essence of philosophy. Russell's emphasis on precision and rigor in the doing of philosophy was derived from his specialized study of mathematics and logic. A short-lived fascination with Bradley was followed by a permanent rejection of his conception of metaphysics as the *'finding of bad reasons for what we believe on instinct'*. According to Russell, even if the reasons were good, philosophy, as a matter of principle, should not be employed as a defense or support for our values and aspirations, but must be a neutral rigorous analysis of statements and facts, in the spirit of science. It should embody the spirit of science, if it wishes to become fruitful and effective. As regards common sense beliefs, Russell refused to accord them the status given by Moore. If science could reject common sense at several points, philosophy could not be refused a similar *Authority* in the name of reason or consistency.

While Moore was absorbed in practicing analysis without any metaphysical worries or ambitions, Russell elaborated his metaphysics of *Logical Atomism* as the theoretical justification of the analysis practiced by Moore and himself. Accepted by Wittgenstein and Wisdom, in their early phase, this *Atomism* finds its purest expression in Wittgenstein's *Tractatus Logico-Philosophicus*.

Facts or objective states of affairs are either simple or complex in varying degrees. But even simple facts have a structure, and contain at least one constituent and one component as their elements. Russell calls the simplest facts *Atomic Facts*. Complex or molecular facts are sets or classes of atomic facts and are reducible to them without any remainder. Propositions express facts. *Atomic propositions* express atomic or simple facts, while *molecular propositions* express complex facts. In an ideal language there is a one to one correspondence between the elements and structure of the proposition and the elements and structure of the fact. The form of the proposition mirrors or pictures the form of the fact. In other words, the grammatical form of the proposition and the logical form of the proposition or of the fact are identical. But natural languages are far from being perfect, and the grammatical form often misleads us about the logical form. This confusion is removed by analysis. A number of philosophical questions and problems arise only as a result of confusion of the logical with the grammatical form.

The calculus of the *Principia Mathematica* is the skeleton of the perfect language. Whatever can significantly be said can be said in that perfect language, without distorting the logical form of facts or propositions. What cannot be said is not significant or meaningful, since the syntax of this language is also the syntax of facts. Violation of the syntax of this perfect language leads to *type* mistakes. Two other basic concepts underlie Russell's conception of analysis they are (a) *logical construction,* and (b) *truth function.*

Logical constructions are constructed out of individual or particular simples to which they are reducible without remainder. Hence, although logical constructions are not fictitious, they are not *real* in the sense in which the simples or particular entities are real. The *average man* does not exist over and above individual men. England is not over and above the individual Englishman, occupying a piece of land. A chair or table, just like a navy or team, is not over and above the particular entities or members composing the whole. They may, thus, be said to be *incomplete symbols* in an important sense.

Ordinary language contains many logical constructions and descriptive phrases, beginning with the definite or indefinite articles. Such employment brings about considerable economy and generality. But since logical constructions and descriptions appear to be just like ordinary names, and are apt to be viewed by us as complete symbols standing for some objective entity, they are a source of confusion. They tempt the unwary to posit descriptive phrases or logical constructions as real constituents of objective facts, or, as parts of the furniture of *Reality.* Analysis enables us to avoid such reification.

Truth-functions are those statements whose truth-value, that is, truth or falsity is a logical function of, that is, logically depends upon the truth or falsity of some other statement. Russell holds common language to be *truth-functional*. That is, the, truth or falsity of all complex propositions is a logical function of some simple atomic propositions or a set of such propositions. Analysis is necessary for exhibiting the *truth-functional* anatomy of complex statements, or, in other words, understanding how they are deducible from the simple statements of which they are truth-functions. These simple atomic statements can be verified. We can thus test the truth claims of complex statements without being misled by their grammatical form.

Thus, functionally speaking, the approaches of Moore and Russell were the same, and led to *new level* or *directional analysis,* even though Moore was indifferent to the metaphysics of *Logical Atomism*. As in the case of Moore, Russell's analysis is a means to the understanding of Reality, or of the ultimate structure of *Being.* The idea of philosophical analysis as the pursuit of meaning as distinguished from the pursuit of truth had not yet been theoretically accepted, even though Moore's approach in practice almost coincided with it.

LIMITATIONS OF LOGICAL ATOMISM & DIRECTIONAL ANALYSIS

According to *Logical Atomism*, significant propositions are either atomic, hence empirical, or truth-functions of atomic propositions. Now the statements comprising the metaphysics of *Logical Atomism* are neither of the two. They do not state facts, but point out the nature of the relationship between facts and language. Hence Wittgenstein admitted them to be nonsense. He qualified his admission by adding that it was *important nonsense*, and that he had *shown* facts, rather than stated facts. Russell, however, does not appear to have made this admission at any stage.

The value of directional analysis was severely limited by implicit assumptions about the nature of language. Wittgenstein brought these assumptions and their consequences to light in his later stage. Here I cannot do better than quote Warnock, *"If our Language had really been, as Russell thought it was, mere meat on the bones of a logical calculus; and if the calculus in question were, as it actually was, quite simply and very rigidly articulated, almost wholly independent of contextual factors, and designed for the special field of fact-stating discourse; then it would have been the case that most of our ordinary expressions could have been properly and even exhaustively analyzed in the narrowly logical, context-neglecting manner adopted by the practitioners of 'logical analysis'.*" See *English Philosophy Since 1900*, page 120.

Since language is neither like a mathematical or logical calculus, nor strictly truth-functional through and through, as assumed by Russell, his directional analysis fails in clarifying and showing the various meanings and functions of language in actual practice. Consequently, it also fails to diagnose the deeper causes of philosophical disagreement.

THE LOGICAL POSITIVIST APPROACH

Logical Positivism was the explicit elaboration of the anti-metaphysical strain of Wittgenstein's *Tractatus*, which had a profound influence upon the *Vienna Circle*. This group came into being in 1922, with Schlick, Carnap, Hahn, Waismann and Neurath, as some of its most prominent members. They were already inclined towards the *Positivism* of Mach and had also been influenced by Russell. But Wittgenstein's *Tractatus* led them to qualify their Positivism as logical. They claimed that it was the product of a logical analysis of the nature of language, rather than of a general predilection in favor of science and mathematics and against metaphysical speculation. Wittgenstein was never a member of the circle. The connecting link between *British analytical philosophy* and the *Logical Positivism of the Vienna Circle* was A. J. Ayer.

Logical Positivism is the most extreme and radical version of the analytical approach to philosophy. It analyses philosophical statements in order to ascertain the type of discourse to which they belong. Linguistic discourse is divided into two sharply different types; cognitive and emotive. Cognitive discourse alone can be said to comprise *statements*. Emotive discourse consists of expressions of attitudes, feelings and emotions, etcetera. Cognitive statements alone are meaningful, since meaning is the relation between a symbol and the symbolized, or between an assertion and a fact or set of facts. Emotive expressions lack cognitive meaning, since there is no factual assertion, but only an expression of the subjects attitudes or feelings etcetera.

Having gone thus far *Logical Positivists* divide cognitive statements into synthetic factual statements and analytic logico-mathematical statements or tautologies. Only these statements are cognitively meaningful. Hence, they alone can be true or false. Emotive expressions may be proper or improper, strong or weak, useful or harmful. But there is no point in calling them true or false. Their emotive meaning must not be confused with cognitive meaning.

Being analytic logico-mathematical statements are true or false by definition. Understanding such statements is enough for understanding their truth or falsity. Factual statements are true or false depending on whether they are verifiable or not. But before they can be true or false, they must be meaningful or intelligible, in the sense that their possible mode of verification must be understood. Thus in the last resort, the meaningfulness of factual statements is linked with or even identical with their mode of verification. Hence the dictum: '*The meaning of a proposition is the method of its verification*'. If a statement lacks a method of verification, it lacks cognitive meaning, and is only a pseudo-statement. It has no cognitive meaning; it can be neither true nor false. It is meaningless or non-sense in the strict sense, even though it may be correct grammatically.

The logical positivist chooses putative metaphysical statements for analysis. Since traditional metaphysicians hold them to be cognitively meaningful, he immediately demands to know the method of their verification. Since, there is actually none, the positivist questions whether some method is possible in principle, even though it may be difficult or even impossible in the physical sense. If the answer to this latter question is also in the negative, the positivist concludes that metaphysical statements are neither true nor false, but meaningless, cognitively speaking.

The traditional metaphysician admits them to be unverifiable. But he still holds them to be cognitive in nature. Cognition or knowledge is always of something, or has an objective referent. The referent of metaphysical statements is metaphysical *Being* or *Reality*. They describe metaphysical facts. Thus the traditional view of metaphysics is that it is a descriptive super-science, and that its statements are cognitive reports of *Reality*. *Logical Positivism* holds that metaphysical state-merits (on the most charitable view) are disguised tautologies and may be partly useful for that purpose. But as putative reports about *Ultimate Reality*, they are non-sense.

Why has this non-sense been perpetuated for so long and still continues to flourish? *Logical Positivism* says that this has been due to a complete neglect of a theory of meaning and typology of discourse as the foundation of philosophizing. This has led to various types of confusions, particularly the confusion of various types of meaning with one another. The lack of a clear cut distinction between the grammatical and the logical form of statements further stood in the way of realizing that grammatically correct sentences nevertheless may be quite meaningless. The formulation of this distinction by Russell and other symbolic logicians went a long way, according to the positivists, to uncover the reason behind the long and hitherto respectable career of metaphysics.

Another basic explanation is the relatively very late emergence in human history of the scientific method. The philosophy of science was an even later product. The lack of a proper knowledge of the nature, functions and criteria of validity of scientific hypotheses conspired to permit metaphysics an honorable existence without impolite enquiries into its credentials. Thus, pseudo-scientific explanations and hypotheses continued to flourish. Metaphysics is essentially pseudo-physics, according to this view.

The logical positivistic analysis is, thus, a typological reduction of a putative statement into one is the two basic types of discourse, cognitive and emotive. It is not a contextual piecemeal analysis. If the putative statement claims to be cognitive, the method of verification is demanded and subjected to analysis. *'What do you mean?'* And *'How do you know?'* Are the recurring refrains of the logical positivist approach.

The summary rejection or elimination of metaphysical statements from the category of cognitively meaningful discourse is an immense relief to the philosopher. He is thereby, released from the, obligation of assessing the truth claims of different philosophical theories and systems. The traditional philosophical theories like Monism, Dualism, Materialism, Idealism, Theism, Psycho-physical Parallelism etcetera or epistemological theories need not be discussed. They are neither true nor false but meaningless.

The liberated philosopher can then proceed to analyze and clarify different concepts, notably those of the natural and social sciences, and study their methodology. Philosophy ceases to be the pursuit of factual truth. It becomes the pursuit of meaning and clarity. The pursuit of truth is handed over exclusively to the body of sciences under the control of the scientific method.

He regards ethical statements *Logical Positivism* holds them to be emotive expressions of one kind or the other. There have been several variations on this theme. For example, ethical sentences have been viewed as prescriptive, or as evocative. But as these views are essentially chips of the same block, they presuppose a sharp and rigid distinction between cognitive and non-cognitive or emotive types of discourse. The most balanced approach is that of Stevenson, Nowell Smith and Toulinin. But since they are linguistic analysts, rather than *Logical Positivists*, their approach is treated in the next section.

THE LIMITATIONS OF THE LOGICAL POSITIVIST APPROACH

The summary elimination of metaphysics from the range of cognitively meaningful discourse on the basis of the Verifiability Principle is invalid. It implicitly equates metaphysics with transcendental Onto-cosmology. But this is not the only conception. Metaphysics, in its other possible conceptions, may be possible, even inevitable. But the logical positivist approach fails in making a balanced assessment of the nature and function of metaphysics, even though it must be credited with finally exploding the persistently held conception of metaphysics as a super-science. In this respect it drives the last nail in the coffin originally prepared by Hume and Kant.

The typology of discourse and theory of meaning which are the points of departure of the logical positivist approach are too crude and incomplete to comprehend the complex logic of ethical, religious and metaphysical statements. The logical positivistic theory of meaning is designed to eliminate these types of discourse, and it is no wonder that they are eliminated when the theory is consistently applied. The typology is, as it were, a rigid and artificially constructed frame containing pigeonholes, into which different statements are fitted. Those which do not fit properly are thrown out as pseudo-statements or meaningless, albeit grammatically correct sentences. Obviously these complex statements are maltreated, and not analyzed or explored, as to how they come to be what they are and what is their function and criterion of validity etcetera. In short, the logic of these statements is totally ignored. This leads to a dogmatic elimination of metaphysics and the impoverishment of philosophy.

The logical positivist approach is unconsciously based upon a number of persuasive definitions of key words like *statement, meaningful, meaningless, cognitive,* and *true* etcetera. This is the consequence of implicit assumptions, notably, a rigid dichotomy of types of discourse, and the superior status of factual discourse, especially the language of natural science.

These limitations will be mentioned in some detail in the section on Linguistic Analysis.

LINGUISTIC ANALYSIS

The approach of linguistic analysis in some respects is similar to the philosophical analysis practiced by Moore. But it is definitely distinct and leads to different conclusions. The greatest single contribution to the formulation and application of this approach is that of Wittgenstein in his later post *Tractatus* philosophical phase. *The Blue and Brown Books*, and later on the *Philosophical Investigations* reflect this new approach. But much before their publication, the oral teaching and discussions held by Wittgenstein had generated a fresh analytical approach that was reflected in the work of Wisdom and Ryle, and many others after them. This approach is accepted now by several distinguished British and American philosophers and is, perhaps, an achievement of our century. It is a growing and vigorous movement and I am powerfully attracted towards it.

The key contention of the linguistic approach is that words of a natural language have a variety of functions or uses, apart from a plurality of meanings. Moore concentrated upon analyzing the various meanings of a word or expression used in philosophical statements, with the view to making them clear and distinct, and thus to resolve philosophical controversies based upon confusion of meanings. Moore did not pay sufficient heed to the various functions of language. Consequently, his analysis could not touch the root-cause of the genesis of philosophical paradox and disagreement. Wittgenstein points out that prior to solving philosophical disputes, their nature must be fully understood. This is analogous, to Moore's theory and practices that prior to answering philosophical questions, or, to use Ryle's happy phrase, *'taking sides in philosophical disputes'*, the exact meaning of the question must be analyzed.

Philosophical questions cannot be settled by observing facts, since in many cases the disputants are agreed about the facts. Secondly, philosophical questions cannot be settled by pure logical methods, or their answers proved with deductive certainty. Had this been the case, philosophical controversy would have ceased, as is the case in the sphere of mathematics and logic. Thirdly, philosophical theories have a paradoxical ring, which makes them appear to be true and false at the same time. We find ourselves saying: It must be the case, but surely, this is not, or cannot be the case. This philosophical perplexity or bewilderment is a typical accompaniment or characteristic of philosophizing.

What, then, is the nature of philosophical disputes and how do they arise? Wittgenstein says that they arise because of an insufficient grasp over the logic of our language, or in more concrete terms, because of our inability to command a clear view of the diverse uses and functions of the words of our language and confusing these diverse uses with one another. This confusion generates puzzles or paradoxes that constitute the body of philosophical theories. Traditional philosophers argue for or against a particular paradox, but ignore the sources of the paradox. Wittgenstein does not argue for or against a philosophical theory, but attempts to uncover the diverse functions of the words in question, in order to expose the underlying confusions that have generated the question or dispute. Such a kind of analysis leads to the dissolution of the problem and of philosophical perplexity.

We all know the diverse functions or uses of words in the sense that we put words to those uses in our ordinary natural speech. But we do not notice these differences, or tend to overlook them while philosophizing. Moreover, although we are familiar with these uses and actually employ words for different purposes, such as, describing, making promises, praising, blaming, joking, and telling stories, etcetera, we are unable to theorize about or recognize these functions in a systematic manner. Hence we are liable to confuse them.

Thirdly, while philosophizing we often employ words, not in their ordinary manner, but we analyze words or expressions to get at their core or essence. Thus, instead of employing the word real by saying that Mr. X's beard or love is not real, we ask: What is the nature or essence of *Reality*? Etcetera.

Let us give some examples of the various functions of words. Words have descriptive, evaluative, performatory, fictional, deductive or analytical, explanatory, exhortative and interpretative uses. This list is only illustrative and not exhaustive. These uses may be mixed in varying proportions. To suppose that because these uses or functions are distinct, they must also be separate is as fallacious and misleading as the view that all words have one essential function, namely representation of some objective entity.

Let us now see how confusing these diverse uses, generates problems. Consider the statements; *'Stealing is bad'* and *'Crows are black'*. In these statements, the words *bad* and *black* are both adjectives. But their function is radically different; in one case it is evaluative, in the other descriptive. All meaningful adjectives refer to some quality. Now if we ignore this distinction, we are at once tempted to raise the following question or questions. What is the meaning of *good*, or the nature of goodness? What is the essence or core of goodness that must characterize all things or states of affairs that are qualified by the adjective *good*? Similarly the adjective *real* may give rise to the question as to what is the essence of Reality? Or, what common features or qualities must a thing or state of affairs possess, if it is real?

Similarly, *'five is a number'*, and *'red is a color'*, are meaningful. Now since colors exist, we are tempted to say numbers exist. The numeral 5, we say, is not meaningless, it must have some objective referent which it symbolizes But since we can never point out the existence of 5, as distinguished from 5 books or 5 chairs etcetera, we are tempted to say that numbers subsist, though they do not exist. Then we may realize, that after all, colors also cannot be pointed out in separation from colored objects or surfaces. We may then be tempted to say that all universals subsist in a trans-empirical non-spatiotemporal realm of *Being*, etcetera. Thus the problems of Nominalism and Realism and Ontological Idealism are generated

Still further, mathematical statements raise the mystery of how pure thought gives us true and certain knowledge about *Reality*. The problems of Kant: '*7 + 5 = 12*' and '*yellow + red = orange*' are both meaningful and true. But the former is true independently of experience, or true *a priori*, while the latter is *posteriori*. We are tempted to treat both as descriptive and synthetic. This immediately raises the problem: How are synthetic a priori propositions possible? But are mathematical propositions synthetic? Is it not the case, that though expressed or formulated in the indicative mood, they only tell us what must be the case if certain conditions are satisfied? '*Either it will rain or it will not rain tomorrow*' does not tell us whether it would rain tomorrow or not. Similarly '*7 + 5 = 12*' does not tell us whether there are seven chairs and five chairs or not, but only that, if there are seven chairs and five chairs, then there must be twelve in all. To ask whether the predicate is contained in the subject is misleading, since the terms of a mathematical equation are not subjects and predicates, in the ordinary sense in which a descriptive statement has a subject or predicate. We must not be misled by grammatical similarities. The '*is*' of predication is different from the '*is*' of an equation or definition. The similarity of grammatical form conceals the dissimilarity of function of words and statements.

The second source of philosophical puzzles or disputes is the temptation to be held captive by selected models or uses of a word in a particular context. We then proceed to make it the standard or Paradigm use. Questions that were appropriately suggested by the Paradigm use or context are then raised in those cases where the word is used in a different context. Such questions generate puzzles. They have no answer. Their destiny is to be dissolved, which constitutes their proper solution. Unfortunately traditional philosophy has attempted to solve them by giving conclusive reasons for or against philosophical theories. For example, we say time is pure movement without anything that moves. But then, what is the speed of time? Motion must have some speed or rate of change. But how are we to measure the speed of time? Again, how can we measure time as such? Time consists of past, present and future. The past does not exist, nor does the future. What does not exist cannot be measured. The present has no duration; it comes into being and immediately merges into the past. Therefore, it too cannot be measured.

The ancient paradoxes of Zeno about Achilles and the tortoise, and the arrow are too familiar to be described. Similarly, we are tempted to say the existence of physical objects or other minds cannot be proved but are merely hypotheses. Wittgenstein holds that all such puzzles and paradoxes arise because we are under the monopolistic grip of a particular Paradigm of the use of a word or expression. We unconsciously extend that model to other contexts in which the word is used. In other words, we make an unconscious generalization about the logic or the rules and mode of the use of a word in the light of a particular context.

Thus, *'measurement'*, *'movement'*, *'proof'*, and *'possibility'*, etcetera, all have a complex logic, that is, they are used in different contexts and for different purposes. We measure time, intelligence, feeling and tables. Similarly, we prove a theorem, a point of law, a scientific hypothesis, an ethical judgment or philosophical interpretation etcetera. If we ask; how can we measure the past, which does not exist? We adopt the use of *measurement*, in the case of measurement of rooms and tables, as our Paradigm case, ignoring other cases, for example, the measurement of the past through the present observable effects of past events or the measurement of intelligence etcetera.

Wittgenstein points out that ordinary words do not, have a single use, and hence no atomic meaning. There is a manifold of use and meaning, and a manifold of rules regulating their use. But there is a family resemblance between their various uses, in virtue of which they are uses or meanings of the same word. But this family resemblance cannot be used to limit the behavior of a word to a sharply demarcated and rigid use.

There is no one logically correct use of a word. But different philosophers or individuals are inclined to make one particular model of use as the standard or Paradigm case, and to dispute with others against other chosen Paradigms. However the business of philosophy is not polemics but conciliation. This is brought about, by pointing out all the various models and the *sources* of the choice of a particular model by an individual, that is, the reasons prompting a person to make that choice. This is repeated for all the different models or theories that exist. This comparative linguistic survey or mapping of the logical geography of words releases the individual from exclusive fascination for or fixation upon a particular model. He is enabled to see the point of each and every rival theory or formulation, and thus conflict is resolved. The grip of a single formulation or model upon the individuals mind is loosened, enabling him to move about freely in linguistic and logical space, instead of being bound or chained to a single Paradigm case. Philosophical perplexity is the symptom of a failure to grasp the logic of language, or more specifically, the variety of the types of discourse and a concrete survey of their functions. The dissolution of philosophical perplexity is the essence of the proper solution of philosophical problems.

Linguistic analysis does not result in the acceptance or rejection of any theory. It is not a preliminary clarificatory activity designed to remove confusion and followed up by the taking of sides in a rational manner. This type of analysis reveals the sources of the conflicting theories and the sources of the question which these theories seek to answer. This insight leads to the dissolution or withering away of the question itself. It is seen as an improper question. An improper question is akin to a *type* mistake pointed out by Russell.

What is the basic cause of this exclusive fixation upon one particular Paradigm use of a word? Wittgenstein was perhaps the first to raise this foundational question and give a convincing answer. He says that the cause is an implicitly held theory of the meaning of word: the *Fido-Fido theory*, as Ryle calls it. It is implicitly held that every single meaningful word must refer to some objective entity or constituent of the objective world. Similarly statements as a combination of individually meaningful words, refer to an objective state of affairs or facts having a determinate structure.

This was the legacy of the *Logical Atomism* of Russell and Wittgenstein in his *Tractatus* period. This theory of meaning with which the correspondence theory of truth is organically linked, inevitably leads to the habit of positing a one-to-one correspondence between words and their objective referents. This habit in turn leads to the above-mentioned pernicious tendency of foisting improper questions.

Why is this *Fido-Fido*, or the object or correspondence theory of meaning so persistent? This is another basic question. If the detection of the sources of the inclination to accept a theory is really effective in dissolving philosophical disputes, this question provides a test case. The correspondence theory of meaning is an illustration of the assimilation of the diverse uses of words to a single Paradigm case. Many words, indeed almost all words that are initially acquired by the child are in fact *Fido-Fido* words. The simple relationship of a one-to-one correspondence between symbol and the symbolized, or the referent and the referend is the only one a child can grasp. The more complex uses of words, for example, modality, negation, definition, implication, generalization etcetera come much later. The correspondence theory of meaning seizes upon one particular use (the earliest and simplest naming use) and makes it the Paradigm case, assimilating all other uses to it. To the question how do words mean or signify, it answers: by '*being names*'. It thereby neglects the other uses, of words.

The logical positivist approach was an attempt to formulate a theory of the types of language. But instead of starting from an unprejudiced examination of the actual types of discourse in the spirit of exploration and understanding, that is, in a purely inductive and empirical fashion, it constructed a rigid typology after a superficial and hasty acquaintance with the varieties of discourse. Its examination of the concrete and detailed features and peculiarities of statements was, not thorough and painstaking. It was unconsciously biased in favor of natural science, whose methods and concepts were taken as the only material meriting a close scrutiny. Hence the approach of *Logical Positivism* was a closed and not an open one. In an important sense it was theoretical rather than empirical.

The *Logical Positivists* divided discourse into cognitive and emotive, and then more or less ignored the task of a thorough delineation and exploration of emotive discourse. The term '*emotive*' is too wide to be of much philosophical use. Non-descriptive or non-factual uses are of so many kinds, that not much purpose is served by dumping them together to rust in the emotive lumber-room. It is true that religious, ethical, esthetic and metaphysical statements are either not factual, or have non-factual components intertwined with factual ones. But to give them all the single label of *emotive* is highly misleading. The logical positivist approach was a wrong step in the right direction.

Metaphysical statements are not to be rejected as non-sense in the garb of correct grammar. They are rather serious challenges to the philosopher to survey the complex logic of the words used in such a statement. Moreover, the inclination to make such statements or the metaphysical temptation, as it were, is not just a bad habit of the philosopher to confuse himself and confuse others with, or to play a game of words. The gap between the grammar and logic of language, and its open texture and flexibility are responsible for this almost inevitable and deep-rooted predilection towards metaphysics. It is a *bewitchment* of our intelligence by language. We are lured into metaphysics by grammatical illusions. The function of linguistic analysis is to put us on guard, and to enable us to see through the tricks language plays on us. This is the *heir to the subject that used to be called philosophy.* This analysis leaves everything as it is and does not give us any fresh knowledge. But by clarifying the diverse uses of words it enables us to command a clear view of the linguistic terrain. It liberates us from the danger of falling into hidden language traps, and thus saves us from the struggle of trying to get out. But perhaps we cannot help being bewitched at times.

How this approach illumines and clarifies the nature of philosophical theories is well illustrated by the manner in which Nowell Smith, Toulmin and others deal with some ethical theories.

It was mentioned previously that *Logical Positivists* differed among themselves as to the exact nature of ethical sentences. Subjective-cum-emotive, evocative and prescriptive theories were put forward in place of the traditional objective-cum-cognitive theory. Nowell Smith and Toulmin hold that ethical statements are neither purely this nor that, but they vary from context to context. It is their concrete use or the function they perform that is the criterion of their nature. They do not have any fixed or rigid nature, whether, emotive or evocative or prescriptive. We are inclined to believe that ethical statements must be of a rigid type precisely due to a wrong theory of meaning implicitly accepted by us.

All reductive assimilations of the diverse uses of statements whether ethical or factual, to one model or use are the consequence of an exclusive fascination or fixation upon some one particular Paradigm or mode of use. This fixation is not arbitrary. There are linguistic and non-linguistic sources of the inclination to get fixated upon a particular Paradigm case. The task of linguistic analysis is not polemical but irenic. Hence Toulmin and Nowell-Smith accept no one particular theory of ethical statements as exclusively true.

Moreover, the sharp division of discourse into factual and emotive statements is no longer acceptable. Many statements are mixed. Thus, to say that ethical statements are emotive is very misleading and also positively false. All that can be said is that ethical statements have an emotive component, without which they would cease to be distinctly ethical. Even this formulation needs to be qualified. But, it is not as misleading as was the purely emotive view, popularized by I. A. Richards, and later on Ayer in their early works.

THE RELATION BETWEEN MOORE AND WITTGENSTEIN

We are now in a position to compare and contrast the linguistic analytical approach with the analytical approach of Moore.

Both are analytical and emphasize the need of clarification. But for Moore, clarification is a preliminary sharpening of the knife, which is supposed to be used later on for cutting metaphysical knots, He may not himself so use the knife because he can not help accepting, or taking seriously the metaphysics or epistemology of common sense. For Wittgenstein, on the other hand, the sharpening of the knife leads directly to the loosening of the knots. Or the problem dissolves in the crucible of analysis. No further surgery is demanded.

Secondly, the nature of the analysis also differs. Moore analyses the various possible meanings of a question or a statement and wants the philosopher to pinpoint his exact meaning. The answer to a question interpreted or understood in sense S_1 would be different from an answer to a question whose verbal formulation is the same, but which is understood in a different sense S_2 or S_3. Failure to distinguish the exact sense of a question, leads to different answers by different philosophers. Prima facie they are different answers to the same question. But really the questions are different in spite of an identical verbal formulation. Thus, Moore's analysis leads to exact and precise questions and answers. This precision either dissipates disagreement, or creates the conditions of overcoming it. It also leads to the possibility of agreement to differ.

Wittgenstein's analysis consists of a survey of the manifold of uses of the words employed in a philosophical theory or dispute. This survey enables us to grasp the logic of those words, and see how questions proper in one context, are erroneously transferred to another context, in which they are improper. We go behind the question, so to speak, and discover it was a futile one.

Moore is interested in analyzing meanings, while Wittgenstein in surveying uses of words and expressions. The latter activity goes behind the former, just as Moore's activity in its own turn goes behind the pre-analytical acceptance or rejection of a philosophical statement. Moore's approach reveals the sources of disagreement up to a point. Wittgenstein's approach powerfully lights up the features of the linguistic territory in which we happen to be moving. We not only see one source of disagreement—namely plurality of meanings behind identity of verbal form, but a far subtler source of confusion and disagreement. It is the assimilation of the plurality of uses of language to one particular use under the influence of the correspondence theory of meaning.

Thirdly, Moore's analysis is sometimes insufficient for separating the logical form or use of a statement or word from its grammatical form or use. This is the result of (a) A limited exploration of the logic of language or the types of discourse, (b) An implicit correspondence theory of meaning. For example, Moore's view that goodness must be the name of an un-analyzable non-natural quality springs from his view that the word *goodness* must correspond with some entity, in order to be significant, which it actually is. It also springs from confusing the grammatically descriptive or indicative form of some ethical statements with their logical form, that is, their distinctive evaluative use.

Both types of analysis dispel disagreement and lead to an agreement to differ. In a sense, both seek to detect differences of meaning concealed by an identical verbal formulation, instead of hastening to give an answer one way or the other. But Wittgenstein's analysis is deeper and more critical, since it attempts a wider survey of the diverse uses of the words in question. This reveals the central as well as the marginal field of use of those words, and the interrelations of those uses. Moore's analysis is confined to the explication of meanings of a question or a statement. Its results are comparatively trivial.

Wittgenstein's insight into the nature of language, his diagnosis of philosophical disagreement and his recommended cure stand to Moore's analytical approach as modern psychotherapy stands to the simple psychotherapy of Coue and others.

The acceptance of Wittgenstein's approach leads to a radical and revolutionary conception of philosophical disputes, and solves problems by preventing them from being formed. They are formed as a result of the confusion of the different functions or uses of words and types of discourse. The philosopher is like a fly-trapped in a fly bottle. Linguistic analysis liberates him. Moore's approach is not so revolutionary. It clarifies the atmosphere and reduces the fog, leading to a better vision.

But it does not reveal the way out of the philosophical maze. Indeed, he was honest enough to admit this in several contexts, most notably the problem of the relationship between sense data and physical objects. The reason of this failure is that it does not illuminate all the twists and turns of the uses of language, but only the twists of the *meaning* of words and statements.

THE LIMITATIONS OF THE LINGUISTIC APPROACH

The linguistic approach holds that philosophical problems are essentially paradoxes generated by an insufficient grasp and hence confusion between diverse functions or uses of the common words of natural languages. Those confusions are removed through linguistic analysis, and *ipso facto* the problems dissolve. This meta-philosophical theory is partly correct, but it becomes inadequate and unsatisfactory if it purports to be all-comprehensive. This approach starts by defining philosophical problems as paradoxical. It is true, that a sufficiently large number of philosophical problems fall, in this category, and can be shown to dissolve according to the linguistic recipe. But several other problems stubbornly refuse to be accommodated in the linguistic framework.

It is significant that Wittgenstein did not formulate this meta-philosophical theory as a result of an inductive survey of the history of philosophy. His samples were taken from his own philosophy or of some selected philosophers, like Russell and Ramsey. It was a pure coincidence that he came across numerous paradoxes and was thus led to generalize about the nature of philosophy.

Wittgenstein is here unconsciously doing what he warns us not to do, namely making a particular example or set of examples into a Paradigm that is used for a generalized theory. He appears to be in the monopolistic grip of a particular set or type of philosophical problems. He never analyzed the cultural or the existentialist approaches to philosophy.

Secondly, his theory of metaphysics does not do justice to the element of *linguistic penetration*, which Wisdom finds in metaphysical statements, besides the element of linguistic confusion. Wittgenstein would have us be cured of metaphysics, while Wisdom night connive at our being lured into it.

Thirdly, he seems to have missed or over-looked the positive functions of metaphysical theories and world views, namely an *existential unification* of the basic features of human experience. Though he analyses the various functions of words and expressions, he does not analyze the function of world views like Theism, Idealism and Humanism, etcetera.

In spite of these limitations, however, he has made perhaps the most outstanding contribution of our times to the growth and enrichment of meta-philosophy. Philosophical problems that do respond to Wittgenstein's linguistic therapy are so many and so scattered, that we must be grateful to his analytical technique.

Phenomenological Analysis

Husserl conceived Phenomenology as the foundation and essence of a rigorous and critical philosophy. The main task of Phenomenology was an accurate description of the pure essence of various phenomena without any admixture of interpretations, assumptions or spatiotemporal particularities. It may thus be called a rigorous *Immanent Ontology* as distinguished from the traditional *Transcendental Ontology* criticized by Kant. Its method was pure reflection or *eidetic intuition*. *Speculative Onto-cosmology* together with its theories of *Idealism, Materialism, Theism, Monism* and *Dualism* etcetera were held to be the product of a pre-phenomenological speculative approach. This resulted in loose and woolly thinking and disagreements, with no method of eliminating them.

All beliefs and judgments were required to be suspended after the fashion of Descartes. This was called the *transcendental epochee*. This procedure was necessary in view of the distortions of the pure essence of phenomena due to conventional and currently accepted beliefs at the level of popular thinking. The intertwining between phenomena and interpretation is the main source of a distorted cognition of the essence and structure of phenomena. *Phenomenological Reduction* seeks to purge phenomena of these assumptions and interpretations. Thereafter pure reflection reveals their essence.

The natural sciences give us factual predictive knowledge, which is indispensable for our practical life and for our controlling the course of events. This knowledge, which concerns phenomena, is precise and accurate. But it is limited to the concrete content of our perceptual experience of an object or set of objects. The abstract, or the purely essential and formal structure of the concrete perceptual experience, is not grasped by experimental science. To the extent that a developed theoretical science like Physics does attempt this task, it becomes phenomenological. But then Physics must shed its assumptions, if it aspires to the status of Phenomenology. It can, however, never supersede Phenomenology, because its area of analysis is limited. Phenomenological analysis has all phenomena under its purview, while the various sciences deal with only demarcated regions. Hence, the necessity of a super and all embracing, phenomenological discipline. This is the base as well as the crowning glory of science. This super-science must not, however, be understood as a *Transcendental Ontology* describing trans-empirical *Reality* or *Pure Forms* existing or subsisting in uncontaminated and glorious isolation from matter. All phenomena according to Phenomenology have an objective as well as a subjective *pole*.

This conception of Phenomenology appears to be strikingly similar to the scientific *Cosmology of Whitehead* or the *Ontology of Hartmann*

THE LIMITATIONS OF THE PHENOMENOLOGICAL APPROACH

The necessity of a rigorous and sustained analysis of concepts and statements, and the questioning of all assumptions, prior to philosophical assertion or argumentation is unquestionable. But the nature and technique of analysis must be correct. Analysis is of different types, and not every type of analysis can be fruitful. Its specific nature is of crucial importance. Moreover, the analyst must not be deceived or misled as to the real nature of his techniques. The real import of a procedural method or technique may be quite different from its intended import. Thus, the philosopher may think he is analyzing or describing the nature of transcendental *Reality*, when he may be analyzing his experience of Reality. He may think he is discovering a priori synthetic truths of reason, when he may be analyzing the implications of conventional or partly conventional definitions etcetera. Finally, it is important to ask whether the type of analysis accepted, presupposes any assumptions or not. If it does, it is essential to make those assumptions explicit.

It appears to me that phenomenological analysis is not as fruitful as it claims to be. Its *meta* conception of its own nature and function is confused. This confusion is due partly to the style and terminology of Husserl, and partly to the general neglect of a theory of language in his time. The types of discourse, their various functions, the theory of meaning, the unconscious extensions of the empirical use of words to a trans-empirical use, were not considered by Husserl. Hence, phenomenological analysis is not as effective for diagnosing and solving the problem of philosophical disagreement and perplexity, as is the contemporary linguistic approach.

Phenomenological analysis can not detect subtle language traps, and thus fails to prevent our falling a victim to various confusions like the confusion of a revisionary or recommendatory use of language with a descriptive use, or the amplification of a tautology with the supposed discovery of meta-empirical facts, or questions of fact with questions of meaning and evaluation.

Husserl's style and terminology are unnecessarily verbose. They fail to give the philosopher a simple yet accurate insight into his own procedures of analysis. He is not giving purely conventional definitions of terms and expressions, as some British and American analytical philosophers are apt to believe. But he is also not describing or revealing the structure of pure phenomena as Phenomenology holds. Stevenson's concept of a persuasive definition appears to me to be the key to the understanding of all such analyses. Phenomenological analysis has both a conventional linguistic aspect, as well as a pure eidetic function. It should neither be unduly mystified nor debunked as a mere fancy-dress show of stipulated definitions or recommendations of usage of words. In any case, the contribution of Phenomenology to the concrete analyses of moral values, and the analysis of the concepts of Philosophical Anthropology by Scheler and others are significant, independently of the validity of the phenomenological theory of philosophy.

Phenomenological analysis does not grasp the necessity and role of world views or conceptual fields for the unification of human experience. It thus, remains unduly restrictive in its conception of the scope of philosophy. The discovery of the pure essences of phenomena is no substitute for the analysis and construction of conceptual fields, just as *grammar* is no substitute for literature. It is certainly wise to restrain oneself unless the logical and situational grammar of world views, together with agreed criteria of their validity has been formulated. But restraint should not lead to indifference.

CHAPTER 6

THE EXISTENTIALIST APPROACH TO PHILOSOPHY

GENERAL INTRODUCTION

The existentialist approach is not entirely new in history. In an important sense Socrates was an existential philosopher, for whom philosophy was not an exercise in abstract speculation and system building, but a systematic and sustained reflection upon the concrete problems of human existence, particularly the problems of the good life. A logician, mathematician or scientist may be deeply engrossed in the solution of some problem. A theologian or philosopher dwelling on the problems of good and evil, God and immortality etcetera is, on the other hand, engaged in existential problems, in the sense that his whole mode of life is at stake. The genuine admission of the existence of God, or the authentic acceptance of a value scale, involve and demand corresponding changes in the mode of being and conduct of the individual. It is true that a scientific theory also leads to action. But this action is concerned with the manipulation or explanation of external spatio-temporal objects, and not with the values, aspirations and hopes of the individual. The peculiar characteristics of existential thinking, *viz*, doubt which can never be definitely overcome, need for commitment, and a total inner integration and transformation of the subject, once the choice has been made, are absent from scientific and mathematical thinking.

Existential questions have an impact upon the attitudes, evaluations, aspirations and responses of the individual to the total environment. Questions of logic, mathematics and the natural sciences, do not have any such impact upon the inmost being or existence of man. Correct factual information provides him with knowledge enabling him to act successfully and satisfy his desires. Similarly, a mathematical or logical calculus or formula provides him with conceptual tools that lead to economy of effort, precision and aesthetic satisfaction. But the core of the individual, his deepest drives and desires, attitudes, hopes, fears and aspirations, are not involved in such conceptual activities. Questions like; what should be my supreme goal in life? Shall I marry and settle down, or shall I devote all my energies to the mission of Communism or Christianity? Shall I pray to God in a moment of crisis or not? Does God exist? Does God respond to human prayer and entreaty? Shall I be truthful and honest in a grossly materialistic society? Should I follow the ethical code of my society? Or of some chosen leader or leaders? Or should I be completely autonomous? What way of life, the aesthetic, the intellectual, the religious, or the ethical or a combination of the above should I adopt? Should free competition or planned cooperation or a judicious mixture of the two be the basis of social organization? Shall I join a political party or religious or ideological association or should I remain uncommitted and independent? These are some of the foundational questions that arise in the life of man. These questions are qualitatively different from scientific questions. They cannot be answered without consulting ones inner voice, as it were. There is no formula for answering them or any specific observation or experiment that would provide the answer. These questions are not factual or logical.

Existential questions cannot be definitely answered. They leave a man perplexed and baffled. But precisely due to this they touch the depths of the individuals existence. An element of faith or commitment, of choice and decision enters into them, since answers to them can never be proved or demonstrated. To accept them and act upon them involves courage and faith that are totally uncalled for in the case of objective truths. It is this subjective or personal commitment that gives them their crucial importance and value in the economy of

The Existentialist Approach to Philosophy

human life. '*Truth is subjectivity*', is Kierkegaard's aphorism for expressing the crucial importance of subjective or rather existential truths as compared with objective or non-existential (factual and analytic) truths. He does not mean to say that all subjective judgments are true. It is only a striking way of pointing out that *truth* in the highest and most important sphere of life can not be pursued in the form of objectively demonstrable statements, but must be pursued in the existential sense, that is, through subjective judgments to which the individual is deeply and authentically committed.

Thus, the realization that the existence of God or his mercy etcetera cannot be demonstrated does not lead to the discomfiture of the existential theist. It is precisely because such beliefs cannot be demonstrated by the nature of the case, that they are valuable and significant.

Many non-existential questions are connected with or rooted in a basically existential problem. For example, the theories of Ontological Materialism, Monism and Dualism etcetera, or the ethical theories of Hedonism, Rationalism etcetera as discussed in European philosophy are non-existential statements. But they are derived from the existential questions: What is the significance and place of myself in this cosmos? How must I relate myself to the universe? Etcetera. The way, in which such existential questions were treated or mistreated by academic philosophy, turned them into non-existential questions, as if they could be answered definitely, and their truth or falsity established. As in the case of analysis and synthesis, existential and essential problems intertwined in human thinking. When, however, existential problems dominate in a thinker, he may be called an existentialist.

According to *Existentialism*, academic philosophy is abstract and general, and gives no importance to the concrete problems of the individual. Concrete problems do not refer to specific problems of individual men and women. No general subject or discipline can undertake this task. What is meant is that the human person as a finite, struggling, hoping, fearing, loving, choosing, or, in short, *existing* being is completely forgotten in the plethora of highly general and abstract questions about *Reality*, perception, truth and meaning etcetera. For example; the questions—Is *Reality* one or many? Is perception of physical objects direct or representative? What is the relation between facts and language? What is the nature of mathematical and aesthetic statements? Is there psycho physical parallelism or inter-actionism? What prevents philosophers from pursuing existential questions as an integral part of philosophy. These technical questions may so grip the attention of academic philosophers as to eclipse existential questions more or less completely.

It may be objected that such practical guidance is not the function of philosophy but of practical ethics. But if philosophers ignore the problems of practical ethics in favor of pure speculative or metaphysical or methodological problems, then the problems of practical ethics will never be tackled at the philosophical plane.

The existential approach to philosophy is, thus, a protest against a purely abstract and conceptual approach which renders philosophy into a technique of analysis or construction of concepts, essences, or words, as the case may be, depriving it of the function of intensifying the individuals awareness of his own deeper self, his Reality as an existing being. The non-existentialist academic philosopher or metaphysician forgets and loses his own self in the attempt to discover the nature of *Reality*. It is a very bad bargain. The existentialist approach restores the individual to a position of pre-eminence as the subject of philosophical reflection in a world where he has been subordinated to the machine on the one hand, and the crowd or society on the other. It is also an attempt to make philosophy the instrument of self-knowledge, or the depth analysis of the human ego, and its transformation through freely chosen values. This makes the existentialist approach to philosophy practical instead of abstract and argumentative

Philosophy as seen from the existentialist perspective has no systematic theories arguments and counter-arguments. The task of philosophical reflection is not analytical, in the theoretical sense, but the awakening or illumination of the individual existence, or *Existenzerhellung* as called by Jasper's.

The Existentialist Approach to Philosophy

Existence and '*to exist*', in the vocabulary of Existentialism, are not synonymous with '*being*' and '*to be*'. A stone or chair is, but does not exist in this restricted sense. Even all men do not '*exist*'. They exist only potentially, that is, they have the capacity or the possibility to exist. People conditioned by group pressures or influence and living at the mass level without discovering their own authentic self, do not *exist*, but only live. *Existence* in this special sense cannot be absolute. No man, no matter how thoroughly conditioned and inauthentic he may be, can be said to be entirely devoid of existence, since at some moments and in some issues his inner attitudes and responses probably do affect his choices. Similarly, a man who exists in this special sense is liable to regress into an inauthentic mass man at times. There is, thus, an existential or *ontological deficiency*, as Marcel calls it in all individuals. *Existenzerhellung* awakens this potential *Existence*.

This task is often sought to be performed through the medium of the philosophical drama, novel, diary or aphorism. Kierkegaard, Nietzsche, Sartre and Marcel employ this medium. Existentialism has, thus, a mystical or religious component, in the wider sense of these terms, no matter whether the existential philosopher opposes or adheres to a religion in the narrower sense. Thus, while Nietzsche and Sartre are anti-religious and anti-Christian, they yet have a religious, flavor. Heidegger is well known for his brand of mysticism. Jasper's clearly transforms philosophy into a kind of philosophical faith or religion, and proceeds to enumerate the cardinal elements of philosophical faith. The religious and mystical elements of Kierkegaard's thought are well known.

European academic philosophy was never subjected to a more scathing criticism, as regards its general aims and methods, than by Nietzsche, Marx and Kierkegaard. The charge of dogmatism leveled by Hume and Kant against metaphysics, is mild chastisement as compared with the overwhelming critique assembled by this 19th century trio. Diverse as their outlook was, they agreed that academic philosophy, by emphasizing or confining itself to general metaphysical and epistemological issues, ignored a set of crucially important concrete existential questions. These questions alone relate philosophy to life. The unity underlying the diverse outlooks of Marx, Kierkegaard and Nietzsche lies precisely in their common opposition to a metaphysical search for the ultimate essence or nature of *Reality* as a whole, conceived as the central problem of philosophy. They, thus, agree with the analytical approach in a very important sense, namely, in ousting speculative metaphysics from the central to the peripheral position, even though their grounds are partly different.

The situational field of the existential approach is closely similar to that of the analytical approach. The ever-growing uniformity in the conclusions of science together with the continuing controversy and diversity in the field of philosophy evokes the analytical, the existential and the cultural approaches, according to the orientation and cultural background of the individual. In each case chronic controversies lead to frustration and despair, and the emergence of meta-philosophical problems. Those philosophers, who are keenly aware of the limitations of scientific and logico-mathematical knowledge, and the importance of moral and religious statements and attitudes, are liable to emphasize the existential approach to philosophy. Those who are more under the sway of science and mathematics emphasize the analytical approach; while those who are inclined to stress the role of a unifying interpretation of human experience as a whole; are liable to adopt the cultural approach to philosophy. All three attempt to dislodge the conception of philosophy as a *super-science*, with a priori speculation as the super avenue to the *sanctum sanctorum* of Ultimate Reality.

We shall deal with the Christian Existentialism of Kierkegaard, the agnostic existentialist philosophy of Jasper's, and finally the ontological existentialist approach of Heidegger and Sartre.

Kierkegaard and Christian Existentialism

The tradition of academic Western philosophy ever since Descartes has been essential as opposed to existential. Descartes started from doubt and affirmed the existence of the self as a conclusion rather than as a premise. This made his philosophical thinking argumentative and rationalistic instead of existential. Just as he gave reasons for the existence of the self or the ego, he gave reasons for the existence of God, the external world including physical objects and other selves. He tried to deduce or prove the existence of these entities, and their inter-relations etcetera, making such problems the core of his philosophy. He was thus led to focus his thoughts upon their essential nature or essence, their *'what'* or content, rather than upon their *'that'* or existence. Even when he reflected upon his own self or ego, he concentrated upon its what or essence, and was led to say that the essence of the mind was thought, while the essence of the body was extension. Now *'thought'*, as an abstract concept, signally fails to capture and to draw our attention to the concrete and differentiated wealth of the modes of human existence or the activities of the self. The self chooses, doubts, loves, reasons, and commits it self, etcetera. To say that all these activities are forms of thought, or that thought is the *essence* of all these diverse activities, prevents us from grasping them in their concreteness, their specific and determinate modes of existence. It is, as if, instead of describing and identifying the concrete features or characteristics of our friends, we just said that they were all rational animals. This might be true as far as it goes; but it would keep us faraway from knowing them in their concreteness.

In a sense all language is abstract and essential. We can never capture the unique individuality and concreteness of our experience through the net of concepts or words. But there are degrees of abstraction. While for certain purposes, a highly abstract statement may be appropriate and illuminating, for other purposes an abstract statement may be totally inappropriate and misleading. Thus, to say that the essence of the *'self'* is thinking, is highly misleading for the purpose of understanding the nature, experiences and concrete history of the self. We are prevented from realizing that the self is not a series or bundle of thoughts, but that the self is engaged in choosing and willing. To choose or will is not merely to think about what is the case or what ought to be the case; it implies both. It is acting, striving, and transforming what is the case.

Again Descartes holds that man is a combination of mind and

body. This raises the problem of the relationship between mind and body. Now these are all essential questions, since the basic aim is to understand the relationship between two universal concepts or essences, that is, thought and extension. Such questions divert our attention from facing problems of values, and of existence. Kierkegaard tries to reverse the point of departure of Descartes, by affirming the priority of the existence of the self, and by maintaining that no proof of its existence is needed. The existences of the self and of the *'Other'* or the world, in the widest sense of the term, are facts of experience, the datum of our thought. To attempt to prove or deduce their existence from or through thinking or through concepts is a misconceived and uncalled for attempt. Such doubts about the Reality of the *'Other'* are pseudo doubts, and the resultant questions pseudo-questions. The basic questions concern the value of the modes of human existence, and the act of choosing a definite mode. In more familiar terms, the important questions are moral, while ontological or epistemological questions are non-existential, secondary and technical. Philosophy should not be permitted to degenerate into a clash of theories about technical questions in the manner of science. It should be concerned with basic attitudes, their structure, and inter-relations and their consequences. Secondly, it should act as a powerful stimulus to make a definite choice. If philosophy does not play this role, then it is not philosophy, but technics.

Kierkegaard was primarily a theologian with a reformed approach towards Natural Theology and Apologetics, reminiscent of St. Augustine and Schleiermacher. He made a clear distinction between scientific or philosophical belief and religious belief or faith. According to him, it is the confusion of one with the other that lies at the back of Natural Theology and Apologetics. Theologians have attempted to establish or prove their beliefs, as if, they were objective beliefs and could be proved through logical skill, provided they tried hard enough. Kierkegaard questioned this all-embracing extension of the scientific or rationalistic attitude to every sphere of life. Faith was not similar to the acceptance of a scientific or factual hypothesis. The belief in God or Christ was not a hypothesis, and hence it was not proper to apply scientific tests of the validity or truth of a hypothesis to such a

The Existentialist Approach to Philosophy

belief. Faith in God was an act of commitment to a *Supreme Being* or *Authority*. One either had faith, or did not have it. But faith could never be created with the help of arguments and proof. The problem was not to prove the truth of Christianity. Indeed, this attempt was impossible, and betrayed an utter confusion between religious faith and scientific belief. The problem was to become a Christian or be a Christian. If one was already committed to God or Christ, then Apologetics was superfluous. If one was not, then Apologetics or Natural Theology could never make one into a Christian, that is, a person fully committed to God. This commitment could come as a result of an intense reflection upon his authentic self that might inwardly and silently be pressing the individual towards a definite choice. The true Apologetics is, thus, the cultivation by the individual of the life of inwardness. Let him listen to the pulsations and whisperings of his authentic self, rather than to the language of verbal creeds and dogmas that may have been poured into his conscious religious education and training. More often than not, they hinder rather than help the traditional Christian in committing himself to Christ. Kierkegaard thus led to a new and powerful movement of Christian philosophy that inspired the theology of Karl Barth, Emil Brunner and others.

According to Kierkegaard, Hegel's philosophy of religion was a monumental edifice built upon a basic confusion of subjective and objective truth, or religious faith and metaphysical or scientific belief. Philosophical truth was not an abstract version of religious truth, or in other words, Christian beliefs and dogmas like Creation, Trinity etcetera, were not the metaphorical or symbolic representations of metaphysical theories, as held by Hegel.

Kierkegaard's penetrating analyses and descriptions of the various modes of human existence, *viz*, the aesthetic-intellectual, the ethical and the religious provide us with profound insight into the concrete nature of the human self. Such phenomenological analysis is the prerequisite of an authentic and critical choice by the individual. These analyses do not and cannot justify a choice. In fact, there can be no justification or proof of the validity of these various modes of living. But without such an analysis, our choice cannot be methodologically defensible. This aspect of Kierkegaard's thought stimulated the secular existential philosophy of Jasper's and Heidegger, and the philosophical Anthropology and concrete ethics of Scheler, Hartmann and others.

The Agnostic Existentialist Approach of Jasper's

Of all existentialists as well as other contemporary philosophers perhaps, Karl Jasper's offers the most systematic and comprehensive meta-philosophy, that aims to do justice to the metaphysical, scientific, and existentialist approaches to philosophy. While his keen interest in methodological problems was a legacy from Kant, his profoundly religious attitude, in the wider sense of the term, was nourished by a close study of Kierkegaard and Nietzsche. He was, thus, uniquely equipped to give a comprehensive and well-rounded picture of the subject matter, divisions and methodology of philosophy, as distinguished from the profound but scattered insights bequeathed by Kierkegaard and Nietzsche.

Jasper's holds that philosophy consists of three activities or functions which have not been clearly distinguished, and which have been mixed in varying proportions in the philosophizing of different philosophers. A comprehensive meta-philosophy must take into account all three, distinguish them clearly and explain their *raison d'etre* and methodology. An exclusive concern with any one function leads to an inadequate and narrow theory of philosophy. These three activities are:

(a) *Weltorientierung* or philosophical world orientation,
(b) *Existenzerhellung* or illumination of human existence,
(c) Metaphysics.

(a) All factual knowledge is empirically derived and must be verifiable according to the requirement of the scientific method. Philosophy cannot claim to add even a single item of fresh knowledge to the body of the sciences. So far he is in agreement with the *Logical Positivists* and other analysts. But scientific knowledge is fragmentary. The philosophical world orientation attempts a unified conceptual scheme in terms of the categories of the sciences themselves. But this world orientation also remains essentially incomplete and lacks the vigorous certainty of logico-mathematical statements. Any attempted unitary world orientation in terms, say, of matter, life, mind, or soul, etcetera leads to antinomies, and is hence, unable to bridge the gap between these concepts or models of world orientation. The task of philosophical world orientation is as it were, to attempt the impossible, and in the process, to grasp the reasons for this impossibility. This prevents us from coming under the sway of fixed and rigid scientific categories.

(b) The need for *Existenzerhellung* arises for Jasper's, because the human individual is something more than can be completely described by any or all of the sciences put together. Man is not only an object among other objects composing the universe; he is also a potential *Existenz* that is, a subject who is potentially free to choose and make himself. Man as a body or qua object grows out of an external cell. But man, as a subject, has the capacity to make himself from within, to evolve into an *Existenz* or inwardly free and autonomous self. This potential *Existenz* is not amenable to the categories of the natural sciences, nor even to the categories of the experimental and descriptive psychology of the West. This psychology describes and inter relates mental processes and attempts to formulate laws of mental phenomena like memory, imagination, sensation, perception, and association of ideas etcetera. But the depth feelings, attitudes, desires, and aspirations, etcetera, in the inmost movements of the soul, so to speak, are left out of its descriptive net. This deep and elusive human reality is accessible only to what may be called existential self-analysis, which can be performed only by the individual himself. A philosopher cannot describe it adequately; he can only help an individual in the process of this self-clarification or illumination. Jasper's has called this activity *Existenzerhellung*. *Existenzerhellung* gives insight in to the authentic, as distinguished from the pseudo-self. Certain situations in the life of man, like conflict between two powerful but opposed desires, moments of extreme danger, sorrow, imminent death etcetera, called '*limit-situations*' by Jasper's, are especially favorable for the activity of *Existenzerhellung*.

(c) There is yet another activity called metaphysics by Jasper's, in which man constructs symbols or *ciphers* of the world, as a whole. This also goes beyond the domain of pure scientific knowledge. This is not knowledge, nor is it phantasm or pure fiction. These *ciphers* or symbolic pictures of *Reality* have a justification or ontological ground, in the sense that the features of the universe or of human experience suggest them. Yet it would be dogmatic to claim any objective ontological validity for them in the absolute sense. Hence no metaphysical theory can be finally and conclusively true. Every theory is a partial perspective of the all-comprehensive *Reality* that transcends those perspectives or symbolic constructions. What is needed is not a fixation upon any one particular theory, but a perpetual transcendental movement of thought, a gliding from position to position. This is not to be construed as an aggregative juxtaposition of perspectives or views, but as an attempt to project a symbolic image and then qualify it.

Jasper's, thus, refuses to be pinned down to any one particular metaphysical theory like Mechanism or Theism or Idealism etcetera. These are complementary ways of symbolizing, or representing the *All Comprehensive* or *Das Umgreifende*, and each way has its own justification as well as essential limitation. However, there can be degrees of adequacy and inadequacy in these various theories. The influence of Kantian agnosticism and the similarity of *Das Umgreifende* with the Kantian '*Thing-in-itself*' should be noted, since these theories do not give us objective knowledge about *Reality*, but are, ways of representing and organizing *Reality* or relating ourselves to it.

Jasper's maintains that the metaphysical quest is meaningful and rooted in an existential urge that cannot be suppressed. But he warns us against the danger of *abstractive simplism* in our metaphysical quest, as happened in the past. He also warns us not to confuse metaphysics with a super-science. If this exposition is correct, then the points of contact of Jasper's approach with the cultural approach should be obvious to the reader. There is also a striking similarity between Jasper's stress upon the unavoidable inadequacy and fragmentation of different metaphysical theories and Wisdom's approach towards the truth or falsity of contradictory metaphysical theories. As already indicated, Wisdom holds that they reveal linguistic confusion and penetration at the same time. He, therefore, neither accepts nor rejects them, but holds them to be simultaneously illuminating or misleading in varying degrees.

The Ontological Existentialist Approach of Heidegger and Sartre

Both Heidegger and Sartre combine the existentialist approach with the ontological, and are thus metaphysicians no less than existentialists. This does not apply to Jasper's and Marcel, or Kierkegaard and Nietzsche. The difference between Moore and Russell in their approach to metaphysics affords an interesting comparison. Moore does not reject metaphysics, but leaves it aside, due to his preoccupation with analysis. Russell deliberately constructs the metaphysics of *Logical Atomism*. Similarly, Jasper's and Marcel do not construct a metaphysical or ontological system. But Heidegger and Sartre do deal with the ontological question. Indeed, the ontological question or the ultimate nature of *Being* is so central in the thought of Heidegger, that he even repudiates the label of Existentialism, first applied to him by Heinemann in 1929. He now maintains that the analysis of human existence or *Dasein* undertaken in his *Being and Time* was a methodological pre-requisite for grasping the nature of *Being*. It is, however, characteristic of both Heidegger and Sartre, that their treatment of the ontological question refers to the themes of *dread, nausea, absurdity, conflict, choice, commitment, freedom* and *Nothing*, etcetera, rather than to the traditional themes or concepts of *essence, idea, Mind* and *Matter*, etcetera. Hence, Heinemann's interpretation was not unjustified.

In what follows I shall deal explicitly with the approach of Heidegger alone, since Sartre's basic approach to philosophy is similar to Heidegger's. This is reflected in the title of Sartre's main work, *Being and Nothingness: An Essay in Phenomenological Ontology.* The differences between the two, both in their *Ontology* and their analysis of human existence, are differences of emphasis and detail rather than of approach. For example, the terms *responsibility, commitment, nausea, absurdity, sadism* and *masochism* etcetera, are either marginal or totally absent from Heidegger's analysis. But the terms, *Being, Nothing, anguish, Dasein* or *Pour Soi* are common. The differences are partly the result of Sartre's confrontation with human degradation and brutality during the last world war. Sartre's approach has, thus, the same merits or demerits as Heidegger's from the meta-philosophical point of view.

A clear and concise exposition of Heidegger's approach to philosophy is difficult, chiefly due to his own interpretation of his main work; *Being and Time.* He himself alleges that no one has understood him correctly. However, for the purpose of this essay, it is not necessary to go in to the detailed contents of *Being and Time.* What is needed is to grasp his conception of the nature and task of philosophy, and the methodology he accepts. For this purpose his inaugural lecture; *What is Metaphysics?* is of crucial importance. He himself states that he does not wish to talk about metaphysics, but to do metaphysics, and that this is the best way of elucidating its nature and problems.

He examines the metaphysical question; *What is Nothing?* and maintains that *Nothing* is neither mere non-existence, nor merely linguistic negation, that is, a conventional mode of expression. *Nothing* is part and parcel of or contained *Being*, which he distinguishes from '*what is*'. Science is concerned only with *what is* but not with *Being* as such. Metaphysics or *Ontology* is concerned with *Being*, and also with *Nothing.* The fact that *Nothing* is not the mere negation of *Being*, or a purely nugatory concept is established through the experience of '*dread*' or basic anxiety. *Dread* is not fear of this or that but an all enveloping and encompassing fear. But fear is always of something; as a mode of consciousness, fear is intentional, as taught by Husserl. Thus, *dread* is the total fear of something. This something is *Nothing* itself. Hence, *Nothing* is not mere non-existence, but something more. But this something more is not determinate, even as *Being* is not determinate. Thus *Being* and *Nothing* are realities that cannot be grasped through sense experience or the categories of science, but only through existential reflection.

All traditional Ontology's are defective, since they view *Being* through the categories of the knowing mind, and hence transform *Being* into *Being* as known by us. He criticizes previous metaphysics as being subjective metaphysics. But he himself does not give any theory of *Being*, apart from saying negatively, that *Being* is not *what is*, and positively that *Being* is *Being*. This is the lesson we have to learn from the failure of others.

Let us now comment on the above exposition. Heidegger does not propound any specific ontological theory, since any such theory would land us into subjectivity, according to Heidegger. It would close the openness of *Being*, and limit the truth of *Being* to the truth of what is. The same remarks apply to *Nothing*. What Heidegger is doing, is to say that *Being* ought not to be equated with or reduced to any one of its modes. This may be compared with Moore's insistence that '*good*' cannot be equated with any other quality, but is a simple, unique and un-analyzable quality.

This is a pertinent reminder to philosophers not to be misled by their analyses and theories. But by itself it does not carry us any further. *Being* as such remains unknown, or, at least something about which we cannot say or communicate to others. If so, what is the point of *Ontology* as a philosophical discipline? If the tautology; '*Being* is *Being and nothing else*', is the sole terminal conclusion or an ontological enquiry then why make the investigation into *Being* the central problem of philosophy. If we can never transcend the categories of understanding and of reason in trying to grasp *Being* then ought not this lead us to the abandonment of Ontology? Or, if the urge towards the grasping of *Being* cannot be suppressed, then some other method should be clearly suggested as is done by Jasper's in his philosophy of the *Comprehensive*, or as it is done by the mystics. But it appears that Heidegger does not proceed beyond a negative or a tautological position.

In his *Being and Time,* Heidegger does attempt an analysis or *Ontology* of *Dasein* or the human mode of *Being*. But as Heidegger himself admits, this cannot be regarded as an *Ontology of Being*, but is only a preliminary study. Thus it is difficult to maintain that Heidegger's conception of philosophy is fruitful. It appears to be self-stultifying. In his book, *Existentialism and the Modern Predicament*, Heinemann says that Heidegger wishes to catch a shadow.

So what is Heidegger doing when he tries to answer the metaphysical questions about *Being* and *Nothingness*? Is he discovering truths not known before? Is he defining words? Is he framing tautologies? In many cases the apparent point or significance of his statements is the product of a grammatical illusion. This illustrates the *bewitchment of our intelligence* by language as Wittgenstein would say. Thus, since *Nothing* and *Being* can be used as grammatical subjects, to suppose that they are also logical subjects or are *'real'* in some sense or other, is to be bewitched by words. Consider the two statements: *'Beauty is not the same as a beautiful object'* , *'Truth is not the same as a true proposition'*. But what is the significance of these true statements? It lies in the fact that words have different uses in our language or are put to different uses. Thus the logic of *quality-words* is different from the logic of *thing-words* like chair or table. Again there are differences within quality-words themselves. The word *Being* differs from both. It has a use, which is different, both from, the use of quality words like *honesty* or *courage* and *thing-words*, like *'chair'*, and *'table'*, etcetera. It is precisely these differences in the use of words, rather than any insight into the nature of *Reality* or essence of *Being* that are revealed by Heidegger's philosophical statements.

No factual discovery about *Reality*, no ontological insight, no value judgment is made when we accept or deny a statement like: *Nothing* is not mere non-existence, or *Nothing* is prior to linguistic negation, and not vice versa. Such statements draw our attention to the contextual use of the words like *nothing* or *negation*, etcetera, and to the features of our experience that underlie the use of these words. This clarification leads to a better grasp of the logic of our language, or to the commanding of a clearer view of the linguistic landscape. Heidegger's interpretation of metaphysics as providing knowledge of *Being*, thus, appears to be uncalled for and unacceptable. Rather, Wisdom's theory of metaphysical statements appears to be the most satisfactory. There is linguistic confusion as well as penetration. The paradoxes Heidegger formulates are neither true nor false, but illuminating and misleading at the same time.

In the postscript to the revised version of his famous lecture; *What is Metaphysics?* Heidegger raises the following three possible lines of objection to his approach and tries to answer them:

(a) His philosophy of *Nothing* is nihilistic; (b) His philosophy of *dread* paralyses the will to act; (c) His philosophy of *pure feeling* imperils exact thinking. These objections may or may not be valid. But they are entirely different from the type of objections raised in this essay. And Heidegger does not meet these objections. The objections he has in view may be due to misunderstanding him. But he nowhere recognizes the meta-philosophical confusions that vitiate his ontological approach. However, in his analysis of *Dasein* or human existence, Heidegger is illuminating and it is precisely this aspect of his work that has been historically influential, and has placed him among the, group of existentialist philosophers.

Conclusion

The existentialist approach possesses a corrective value. Traditional metaphysics diverted the attention of man from the pressing problems of his own existence. The existentialist approach attempts in its own fashion, to unite philosophy and life, like the cultural approach of Dewey and Dilthey. But it has its own limitations.

No philosophical approach that fights shy of linguistic analysis can be free from serious confusions and fallacies. Unfortunately analytical and existentialist philosophers seldom communicate with each other. Purely analytical philosophers become narrow in their scope and vision, and their approach tends to become a technique, doing scant justice to the depth and range of human experience. On the other hand, existentialist philosophers tend to fall in language traps, and the confusion of vagueness or ambiguity with profundity or comprehensiveness.

The existentialist approach, in spite of claiming to be a concrete approach, ignores the historical determinants of the human personality. It tries to grasp man as a unique individual. But man is both unique and culturally conditioned by the group and the age. He cannot be understood in isolation: Heidegger's concept of *Dasein* no doubt implies that man is there, or is thrown into a situation. But he does not deal with the situation in a concrete way. He loses his path in abstract words, failing to do justice to the concrete historical and cultural determinants of *Dasein* or human existence The reader is referred to a penetrating article; *On the Pseudo-concreteness of Heidegger's Philosophy* by G. Stern in the journal, *Philosophy and Phenomenological Research, 1947-48*. To my mind, however, there is no impediment to the fusion of the existentialist and cultural approaches to philosophy, and indeed of these two with the analytical into a multi-dimensional approach. This subject has been dealt with in the conclusion of this work.

CHAPTER 7

CONCLUSION

Our survey of the different approaches to philosophy is now over. This survey does, not pretend to be complete either historically, or theoretically. Some specific approaches like *Pragmatism* and *Historicism* have not been treated independently, getting only a bare mention as particular versions of the main approaches described in this monograph. But this, I trust, would not affect the validity of the general approach followed in this essay.

The various approaches to philosophy are not arbitrary choices of the individual philosopher, but are situationally evoked. They grow around a particular nucleus or cluster of problems arising from the situational and conceptual fields of the philosopher. They follow a logic, in the sense in which Hegel claimed the history of philosophy to be a rational dialectical movement, rather than a mere succession of theories or systems. The cultural approach could not have crystallized in the early phase of philosophy, just as the analytical could not have preceded the metaphysical approach, or the metaphysical could not have preceded the *'religious approach'*. The logic of the contemporary situation now demands a meta-philosophical multi-dimensional approach as the foundation of concrete philosophizing. This is necessary because the past failure of communication between the different approaches encouraged a polemical rather than an irenic attitude on the part of their protagonists. The elements of truth embedded in them were in consequence ignored in the dust of polemics.

This however, did not prevent an intertwining of these approaches in the actual philosophizing of philosophers. The pure metaphysical, the analytical and the existentialist approaches are all thus, ideal limits, rather than exclusive modes of philosophizing. Russell, for example, is both analytical and metaphysical, while Heidegger and Sartre adopt the existentialist and the metaphysical approaches in the same breath. Socrates combines the analytical and the existentialist approach. The intertwining of the speculative and the *'religious approach*e's has also been mentioned.

Are these approaches compatible or incompatible? They are not only compatible but also complementary, and ought to be fused into an organic multi-dimensional approach. Let us see how these various approaches complement each other, and how each is incomplete or fragmentary in isolation from the rest.

The metaphysical approach in the sense of a transcendental *Ontology* has been shown to be methodologically impossible. But a metaphysical world view as a systematic conceptual field for organizing and interpreting the basic features of human experience has been accepted as not merely possible, but as indispensable. Metaphysics, in this sense, is not only compatible with analysis, but it demands rigorous analysis of the exact structure of the different conceptual schemes and of the concepts that they incorporate. Confusions of meaning, ambiguity, an insufficient grasp of the truth conditions and implications of statements etcetera are thus declared by Moore to be the principal causes of philosophical error and disagreement.

Moore, as already stated, never rejected Metaphysics, while Russell actually propounded one. Wittgenstein, the ancestor of the Non-sense-theory of metaphysics, which was literally accepted by the logical positivists, eventually gave it up in his post *Tractatus* phase. However, he could never endow it with the significance and importance attached to it by the cultural approach. He held that metaphysical statements and paradoxes, though not non-sense, were nevertheless tile product of linguistic confusion, and of the bewitchment of intelligence by means of language. Thus according to him, metaphysics had to be outgrown or outwitted, and not deliberately cultivated. To this extent there is a definite conflict between the cultural and metaphysical approach and the linguistic analytical approach. But this, conflict is only on the plane of theory. The practice of Wittgenstein is perfectly compatible, nay, preeminently useful for metaphysical analysis and construction. Wisdom's significant amendment to the effect—that metaphysical statements are the product, not merely of linguistic confusion, but also of linguistic penetration, and hence are defensible—is an admission (albeit somewhat grudging) of the value of metaphysics. This admission removes the theoretical conflict between the linguistic approach and the metaphysical approach. Whether linguistic philosophers actually do any metaphysics or not is beside the point.

The same remarks apply to the existentialist approach. *Existenzerhellung*, as Jasper's has shown, is a distinct activity. Philosophers may or may not have undertaken this task. But there is no conflict between this task and that of metaphysics or analysis. Analysis would be of definite help in this task. Similarly, *Existenzerhellung* would be relevant to the construction of a comprehensive world view. Indeed a world view constructed without taking into account the results of existential analysis of the individual would be superficial, precisely because of this omission. A comprehensive world view must embrace all the basic features of human experience. The deepest attitudes, aspirations and responses of the individual must, therefore, be identified and described.

The *Ontological Existentialism* of Heidegger and Sartre, in so far as it is an avowed transcendental *Ontology* or metaphysics, criticized by Kant no less than by the *Logical Positivists*, is in a different position. But Heidegger's analysis of *Dasein* or human existence seems to be quite compatible with the analytical approach. The application of the powerful tool of linguistic analysis to Heidegger's analysis of *Dasein* would reveal linguistic confusion as well as linguistic penetration. For too long have statements of the type; *'the cat is on the mat'*, stolen the analytical show from statements of the type; *'freedom is the recognition of necessity'* or *'dread reveals nothing'*, etcetera.

Logical and linguistic analyses are necessary and inevitable, but not sufficient. They must be supplemented by conceptual field analysis. While the analytical approach is usually confined to linguistic or logical analysis, the cultural approach underscores analysis in this wider sense. Such analysis must precede the attempt to answer questions that arise within a conceptual field. But since a conceptual field or philosophical interpretation contains either explicitly or implicitly an evaluative component, conceptual field analysis must itself broaden out into, what may be called, situational analysis. This embraces the analysis of the total situation of the philosopher, including his value system and personality needs.

This alone can lead to that intellectual honesty and dispassionate thought that has long been the philosophers ideal, but seldom realized. It is a superficial view that mere logical sharpness or factual knowledge suffice to suggest a valid conceptual field in the domain of philosophy. Like language, the conceptual field of an individual is, to begin with acquired through cultural conditioning. This may be called the *'mother field'* or the *'in field'*. The individual is attached or fixated upon it. This renders it difficult to grasp other actual and possible out-fields. Mere logical sharpness or factual truths do not suffice to break the natural resistance to the acceptance of out-fields. Inertia, pride and ignorance of the subtle role of the *in-field* in catering to the powerful yet hidden personality needs molded by the group stand in the way of a critical choice of a new field. *Field blindness* and *figure* or *field rigidity* render him unwilling or unable to alter the perspective. Situational and functional analysis overcomes what may be called the ethico-epistemic resistance of the individual at the pre-critical level.

The study of different conceptual fields and value systems emancipates the individual from a pre-critical and externally conditioned monopolistic grip of a particular field. One can then view the world from different perspectives. But one must adopt some perspective after critical reflection. Otherwise, he would become conceptually uprooted or a gliding philosopher in Jasper's sense. A person may know a number of languages well; but he must select a particular language with its rules of grammar and syntax, if he wishes to communicate.Must

Conclusion

we choose a conceptual field or world view? We may consciously and theoretically avoid a definite choice. But we must live as if we had committed ourselves one way or the other. To the extent we do not consciously choose, our personality lacks integration and a direction of movement within conceptual space. Conceptual growth or the evolution of concrete conceptual patterns within a basic conceptual field is stopped or impeded for lack of a creative impulse and a definite direction. This lends to cultural impoverishment and stagnation.

The steps of the correct procedure for choosing a valid conceptual field are briefly as follows:

(a) Distillation of the *empirical manifold* or set of facts from the *interpretative matrix* or conceptual frame.

(b) Linguistic analysis of the terms and concepts employed to display their concrete uses and functions in different contexts, together with their rules of use, or their logic. This is meant to pinpoint the intended use of terms in the context under consideration, and to eliminate *type* confusions and pseudo questions etcetera.

(c) Situational analysis of the conceptual field or fields in question, to reveal the implicit value system of the individual as well as the situational evocators (in Mannheim's language, '*determinants*') of his thought.

(d) Functional analysis of the conceptual field or fields in question, leading to a final choice of a valid field on the basis of the criteria of simplicity, comprehensiveness, consistency and pragmatic fruitfulness.

However, it must be pointed out that there can be no one approach or method that will work in all cases. Situational and conceptual field analysis will do in the case of Theism, Humanism and Idealism etcetera, but probably not in the case of Whiteheads cosmology or Ontology. Linguistic Analysis will certainly work in all cases. But without field analysis, it will not be complete, since the distinctive nature and function of the world view would escape the net of the analytical attack. A definite method, rigidly and invariably followed, would be like confining ourselves to a single tool in the face of different operational tasks.

The choice of a valid conceptual field on the basis of the criteria suggested is ultimately a function of reflection and not of investigation of facts. Thus the possibility of eventual disagreement between philosophers cannot be eliminated, even though the choice is not arbitrary. Two persons may agree to the rules and yet differ in their application. Philosophical disagreement is thus unavoidable. No approach can eliminate disagreement without any remainder. But the type of disagreement that remains on the multi-dimensional approach would be the unavoidable minimum like the unavoidable minimum friction of a well-constructed and well-oiled machine or moving body. It would be a fraction of the disagreement that results from a non meta-philosophical or a mono-dimensional approach.

The disputes about the nature and tasks of philosophy are a function of a one sided fixation upon selective paradigms of philosophical questions and answers. The monopolistic grip of selective instances of a general concept is a fairly widespread phenomenon. Marx's theory of the determinants of social change, Freud's theory of the determinants of neuroses, the different theories of truth or of knowledge, the different theories of the nature of ethical judgments etcetera are all reminders of how the fondness for particular instances or Paradigms leads to a general theory concerning the subject matter. Rather than accept or reject any particular theory of philosophy, we must try to see how far it is illuminating, and how far misleading.

The cultural approach to philosophy attempts to show in what respects and how far philosophical theories and systems or world views resemble the products of affective culture. This approach is illuminating, since the traditional conception of metaphysics assimilates it to the products of purely cognitive culture, like science and logic. This conception renders metaphysics a super-science. But philosophy is neither purely affective nor purely cognitive. Any reductive view would be one sided and partial. Logic and methodology are as much limbs of philosophy as are world views. Philosophy is neither cognitive nor affective culture. It is a multi-dimensional culture of human awareness, inclusive of knowing, feeling and willing.

Conclusion

The multi-dimensional approach attempts to combine, say; Moore's or Wittgenstein's passion for clarification and precision with Jasper's or Marcel's insight into the human situation. This however, does not mean that every philosopher must give equal attention to each and every dimension. The multi-dimensional approach simply protests against the fallacy of simplism, no matter in what form it crops up. The linguistic theory of philosophy and philosophical disagreement is as much one sided as the cultural or existentialist approaches when they are viewed in isolation. The part can never be the whole.

Essay 1

Knowledge And Truth

The traditional philosophical problem is: What is the nature of knowledge/truth? This question assumes (a) there is an essence of truth and knowledge, and the correct answer is one, which grasps this essence, and (b) the different theories of knowledge/ truth are rival answers, only one of which could possibly be the right answer. Thus, for example, if the question concerns the origin of knowledge, then either empiricism or rationalism or intuitionism is the true answer; if the question concerns the nature of knowledge, then the true theory of knowledge is one which captures the distinction between knowledge and belief or knowledge and opinion, since knowledge implies awareness of the grounds of belief over and above true belief. Likewise, truth is either correspondence of statement with fact, or truth is mutual coherence of a system of beliefs, or truth is utility, etcetera.

The classical theories of knowledge and truth are all rooted in the more or less unconscious assumption that all meaningful words, as descriptive '*Fido-Fido*' names refer to some object or entity. These objects may be physical or they may be mental or spiritual, but they must be entities, all the same, having some features, which the philosopher attempts to discern by reflection or non-experimental enquiry. While chairs, trees, animals, matter, energy, motion, and space are physical; goodness, truth, love, and justice are non-naturalistic entities. According to this line of thinking, philosophical theories are cognitive truth claims about the ultimate nature of entities or of *Reality* as a whole. In other words, philosophy is a super-science of *Noumenal* objects or entities as distinct from science, which deals merely with their spatio-temporal appearances.

Logical Positivism went to the other extreme that philosophical theories were either nonsense or at the most poetic expressions of some sort, which were neither true nor false. It seems to me there was a germ of truth in this insight, which was, however, a distorted vision of the nature and function of philosophical theories. It is true that philosophical theories are knowledge claims without being true or false in the sense in which scientific or logico-mathematical knowledge claims are true or false. But the perfunctory dichotomy of discourse into cognitive and emotive and the Positivists' hasty dumping of poetry, metaphysics, religion and morality under the shapeless umbrella of *emotive discourse*, without going into the concrete structural and functional differences between different families of emotive discourse (*viz*, the poetic, the ethical, the aesthetic, the religious, the metaphysical) led to the superficial rejection of classical metaphysical and epistemological theories.

It was John Wisdom who later on pointed out that philosophical theories are a paradigmatic fixation under the over-powering grip of selected instances or uses of a concept. If so, there cannot be any one true theory of knowledge, or of truth or of *Reality*, but only an awareness of the reasons or factors which incline one in favor of this Paradigm or that. This meta-theory of philosophy implies that every philosophical theory is illuminating and simultaneously misleading. A theory is illuminating because it draws our attention to certain features of our experience; it is misleading because it makes us ignore some other features of our experience under the influence of the selected Paradigm. The Paradigm is chosen because of some aspect or feature of our experience, which feature then serves as the norm for identifying, describing, classifying, or grading *Reality* as the case maybe. Now a choice of the norm can be happy, or unhappy, reflective or impulsive, balanced or lop-sided, but never true or false. A choice could be true or false only in the case of applying the norm for identifying objects on the basis of agreed criteria. But when the choice concerns the criteria themselves, the choice cannot be said to be true or false, but only wise or unwise, and happy or unhappy, etcetera.

If the above analysis be correct and if philosophical theories flow from paradigmatic fixations upon a particular feature or set of features of *Reality*, as pointed out by Wisdom, philosophical theories never will be settled or clinched, just as ethical, aesthetic or religious truth claims can never be clinched. If we crave for agreement among all observers or thinkers, we have to give up the game of philosophy as distinct from science. But this agreement would amount to the silence of the grave. Wisdom is right when he says that philosophical confusion as well as penetration is the destiny of the metaphysician. In a way resembling the poet's, the metaphysician does not describe Reality, but enables us to see it in the light of a favored Paradigm, which reveals and yet conceals the complexity of Reality and also the flexibility and range of our language. In the idiom of Wittgenstein, philosophical theories are alternative language games and hence optional rather than compellingly true or false theories or knowledge claims.

In the light of the above meta-theoretical preamble let us now examine the classical theories of knowledge, rationalism and empiricism, and also the contemporary theory of emotivism. We shall then proceed to examine the classical theories of truth, correspondence and coherence, and contemporary theory of redundancy.

Rationalism is a theory of the origin of knowledge and also of the nature of knowledge. In the first sense rationalism states that all knowledge has its origin in reason, or that reason is the source of all knowledge as distinguished from mere sensation or opinion. Let us see what features of Reality (in this case of knowledge) incline us to this view, and thus function as the Paradigm of knowledge. Obviously, the Paradigm of knowledge (in this case) is our cognition of logico-mathematical truths. Even though such truths are initially learnt in the context of perceptual experience, the fact is that these truths, as formal deductive explications of initial postulates or definitions, are independent of perceptual experience. In other words, it is reason and not perception, which is needed for grasping the relations between ideas.

A different Paradigm of knowledge, which may be said to incline us to the rationalistic position, is ethical/aesthetic beliefs, which require insight or intuition apart from sense perception. In the absence of moral insight a cold-blooded murder is a mere physical event; in the absence of aesthetic intuition a divinely beautiful sunset is just an optical illusion. Now, is it not very tempting to hold that not only the grasping of logical connections or relations, but also the intuiting of ethical and aesthetic qualities is the function of reason, which has different dimensions?

Let us now refer to a feature of our knowledge, which gives further support to the rationalistic theory of the origin of knowledge. This feature is the role of reasoning in sorting out veridical from non-veridical perceptions, that is, illusions, and also the role of reason in interpreting the data provided by sense organs and in distinguishing perceptual appearance from objective reality. This point, however, brings us to rationalism as a theory of the nature of knowledge. *Prima facie*, sense experience does not involve the use of reason, at least in the case of veridical perception, which appears to give us knowledge without any reasoning or conceptual interpretation. But is it not the case that even simple veridical perceptual judgments like, '*This is a book*', or '*I see a brown patch over there*', are not reducible to bare sensation but involve concepts and, thus, the use of reason? If so, it becomes true to say: *No reason, no knowledge.*

Having seen why we are inclined to accept the rationalistic theory of knowledge, let us see how, at the same time, it misleads us, on account of which we become inclined to reject it and, thus, land ourselves into perplexity. Beliefs about matters of fact are, in one sense, qualitatively different from logico-mathematical beliefs, *viz*, that the truth of the former is contingent and not necessary. A true factual belief describes an actual state of affairs, which, however, could have been different

Essay 1: Knowledge And Truth

without involving any contradiction. A true logico-mathematical belief, on the other hand, asserts a necessary connection between ideas, and this connection could not have been different without involving an inherent contradiction. When this is the case, beliefs about matters of fact fall in a different class from logico-mathematical beliefs. Factual beliefs, if true, are true because they correspond or agree with (in some sense or other) with an actual state of affairs, and not merely because they are just free from any internal contradiction. Again, the question whether a belief that is free from internal contradiction (in other words, logically possible) is factually true, can only be known through experiencing the actual state of affairs and not through exploring the realm of possibility alone. Whether or not, round squares exist can be known by reflection alone, but not whether tigers run faster than lions. It is precisely this feature or fact, which is ignored when we say with the rationalist that all knowledge requires the use of reason or comes from reason. Likewise, it is precisely this feature or fact, which grips the imagination of the empiricist and inclines him to say that all knowledge comes from experience, including logico-mathematical truths, which originate in experience, even though not constituted by it.

Let us now turn to the contemporary controversy whether ethical/religious discourse is cognitive or emotive, or are the terms *'true'* and *'false'* applicable to ethical/religious beliefs. As in the case of the classical theories of knowledge, the theory of emotivism is both illuminating and misleading. There is thus no need to affirm either emotivism or cognitivism to the exclusion of the other. Rather we must show how and what each reveals and also conceals.

In ordinary language we refer to ethical knowledge or ethical truths. We say for instance; *'I know rape is immoral'*, *'I believe free love is permissible'*, *'I hold mercy killing is moral in such and such cases'*. Now such judgments are qualitatively different from judgments of fact and judgments of reason or implication, since ethical beliefs can be proved neither inductively nor deductively. On the other hand, ethical/religious judgments are also qualitatively different from judgments of taste like, *'I prefer my coffee cold'*, or judgments of attitudinal preference like,

Essay 1: Knowledge And Truth

'I don't like poking my nose in others affairs', or *'I prefer the security of government service to the glamour of politics'*. Nevertheless, judgments of taste, judgments of attitudinal preference and ethical judgments all resemble each other in that they all express the response of the person to an actual or imagined situation, rather than describe the elements and structure of a situation. But while judgments of taste claim to be the subject's response without any claim to universal validity and without evoking feelings of disapproval or indignation at a contrary taste, and without evoking the urge to propagate and establish one's own taste, attitudinal and ethical judgments have an obligatory air about them in varying degrees. Even aesthetic judgments are not so permissive as judgments of taste. We may say there are degrees of permissiveness or of obligation, with judgments of taste at one end of the scale and judgments of morality at the other, with other types of judgments lying at different points on the scale. Yet, all such judgments, which may be called '*judgments of response to a situation*' rather than '*judgments of description of a situation*' have the common features of human choice, variability and non-coercive validity.

Now if we antecedently accept that the definite absence of the above features is the *sine qua non* of a knowledge claim, it will analytically follow that ethical/religious knowledge claims are not *'really'* knowledge claims, but only appear to be so due to our popular beliefs, language habits, confused thinking, etcetera. But the question arises: why should we give the above restricted sense to *'knowledge'*, when ordinary language uses *'knowledge'* to cover our firm ethical convictions, say *'murder is immoral'*, or *'love is good'* and *'jealousy bad'*, etcetera?

No compelling reasons in favor of this restricted use of 'knowledge' can be given, though it is a valid reason (as far as it goes) that ethical/religious beliefs can never be proved, but are condemned to remain controversial by the very nature of the case. This is a pure epistemological reason and is valid without being conclusive. We could also give the utilitarian reason that, denying the status of *knowledge* to ethical/religious beliefs helps to curb dogmatism and promotes the agreement to differ. On the other hand, there are equally valid epistemological as well as utilitarian reasons against the restricted use of

Essay 1: Knowledge And Truth

knowledge. The epistemological reason is that the clarity and certainty of, at least, some basic ethical convictions are as compelling as those of logico-mathematical truths, even granting that the certainty of ethical judgments is existential and not logical. The point to note is that in preferring love to hatred, or in preferring gratitude to one's benefactor to ingratitude, one is not free in the sense of choosing, say, one color rather than the other, but that one chooses under an existential, if not logical, necessity. The utilitarian reason against excluding ethical/religious beliefs from the connotative or denotative umbrella of *knowledge* is that such exclusion demotes the status and significance of ethical/religious beliefs or convictions, as compared with science and mathematics, which become our paradigmatic fixations. It, therefore, seems to me that no compelling or conclusive reasons can be advanced for or against the emotivist theory of ethical/religious judgments.

It is much more fruitful to analyze the different types of models of certainty and of knowledge, according to the ordinary use of language, and also to analyze the sort of verification, generally deemed to be adequate for that model of certainty and of knowledge. This neutral analysis of our actual use of the words '*knowledge*' and '*certainty*' will reveal the different models of verifiability in actual practice, and also show which models are applicable in principle to the different types of '*knowledge*', as the word is actually used in our living language. We will find that scientific knowledge is verified in a different way from logico-mathematical knowledge, or, in other words, the Paradigm of verifiability in the two cases is different, and that scientific knowledge is incapable of deductive or logical proof. If so, why should we not accept yet another Paradigm or model of verifiability for ethical/religious knowledge claims?

A particular model of verifiability must first be applicable, in principle, to a putative knowledge claim before we can properly declare that the knowledge claim falls short of the Paradigm of knowledge. Only if the demand for a particular mode of verification is applicable, in principle (or makes sense in a particular context of human experience), but the verification is actually lacking, could we say that there is an inadequacy or lack in the evidence necessary to convert a belief into knowledge. If, however, we antecedently fix upon a particular Paradigm of verifiability as the essence of verification without which no belief can claim to be knowledge, and we then withhold the status of knowledge from all those beliefs or knowledge claims to which the Paradigm is avowedly not applicable, we, in effect, become captive to a particular Paradigm of knowledge or of verification. We forget that, though the choice of a Paradigm has a logic, this logic is merely persuasive, and not coercive. If we realize this, we will admit that there can be no '*the*' correct answer to the questions: (a) are ethical/religious beliefs knowledge claims? And (b) is ethical/religious discourse cognitive or emotive?

Another reason why neither emotivism nor cognitivism can be accepted without qualifications is that there is a basic difference between ethical judgments concerning instrumental and intrinsic values. All ethical judgments which state that such and such acts, motives, situations are good or right in the instrumental sense implicitly postulate or imply an intrinsic value and then go onto claim that intrinsic value is promoted by such and such acts or situations. Now the latter part of this complex ethical judgment is a factual truth claim. In other words, there is a putative factual base supporting the validity or truth of the total ethical judgment. Now the emotive theory conceals or ignores this factually verifiable base in the case of instrumental values; likewise, cognitivism conceals or ignores the element of the subject's response or valuation in the context of intrinsic values. Valuation, as a response to an actual or possible situation, rather than the description of an actual or possible situation, can never be true or false in the sense of correspondence or non-correspondence with an external situation or an objective truth. Valuation could be said to be true or false in this objective sense (as already pointed out in the preamble) only in the context of either identifying or grading objects, acts or situations in accordance with previously accepted or given criteria. But valuation in the context of freely choosing the criteria of value themselves cannot be true or false, but only wise or unwise, happy or unhappy, authentic or inauthentic, reflective or impulsive, and balanced or lop-sided, etcetera.

Essay 1: Knowledge And Truth

Let us now deal with the classical theories of truth in the manner we have adopted for the theories of knowledge. Each theory of truth fits very well a particular range or type of data, but it breaks down if it is extended beyond that range. For example, the correspondence theory of truth fits factual truth claims, but not logico-mathematical, while the coherence theory is in just the reverse position. The same remarks apply to the controversy between Austin and Strawson concerning the redundancy view of '*truth*', or the expression, is true. It seems to me, there is no single context or use, which could claim to be '*the*' right or proper meaning or use of the expression *is true*. Let us see this in some detail.

Consider the sentence, '*It is true that London is the capital of UK*'. Here the expression '*It is true*' is used in a factual context. But in the sentence, '*It is true that 10 is not divisible by 3*', we use the expression '*is true*' in the conceptual context without implying any actual states of affairs. In this case, how can it be said that the truth of the statement implies correspondence between the statement and facts, or that the statement is true because it corresponds with facts, when the statement merely asserts a necessary relation between ideas. We may say the statement corresponds with laws of logic or mathematics. But then, what is the difference between correspondence with the laws of logic and coherence with other true statements? Does not the difference between the two theories of truth turn out to be merely verbal, at least, in the case of logico-mathematical statements? It seems to me that in the context of logico-mathematical discourse the criterion of correspondence merges into that of coherence, while in the context of factual discourse, the criterion of coherence inevitably merges into that of correspondence with facts. Consequently, we can never claim that one theory or the other grasps the essence of truth more than the other. As long as 'truth is used in both factual and logical contexts, no particular Paradigm of use can be accepted as universally applicable.

Let us examine a more complex type of factual statement, say, '*The average Chinese male is shorter than the average American female*'. Now we can never point out the *average* Chinese or American.

However, the statement is true, only if it corresponds with facts, and false if it fails to do so. But the sense in which the statement could possibly correspond with facts is quite different from the direct correspondence of the statement, say; '*The Qutab Minar is X feet high*', with the actual fact. Average heights, speeds and incomes, etcetera, do not exist in the direct sense in which the *Qutab Minar* exists. Hence although statements containing expressions like '*average height*', '*the intelligentsia*, '*the modern mind*, '*electron*, '*honesty*', '*democracy*', and '*the unconscious*', etcetera, (if and when true) do correspond with facts, this correspondence is no longer a simple one-to-one relation, but a complex relationship which includes both correspondence with facts and coherence with other true statements.

Let us now refer just in passing to William James pragmatic theory of truth. This theory confuses the question of the nature of truth with the question of the test of truth. It also equates the concept of truth with the entirely different concept of utility. James also goes wrong in holding that not only the truths of religion and morality but also the abstract explanatory theories and concepts of science have no justification apart from their utility, Peirce's conception of operational meaning and verification is very illuminating, but it fails to clarify and illumine the nature and function of ethical/religious discourse. Thus, all the classical or traditional Western theories of truth break down in some respect or the other.

Let us now examine the controversy between Austin and Strawson concerning the '*redundancy view*' of the expression '*is true*'. Strawson says that the statement; '*It is true that London is the capital of UK*', asserts nothing over and above the statement, '*London is the capital of UK*'. From this he infers that the expression '*it is true*' does not describe any attribute, quality or relation of a sentence or statement, whether of correspondence or of coherence. Strawson says that the expression '*it is true*' is grammatically similar to the expression, say, '*it is blue*' or 'it is soft. Now since the above expressions do attribute a specific quality or attribute to the noun corresponding to the pronoun '*it*', the expression '*it is true*' also seems to attribute the quality of truth to the corresponding substantive statement. But the expression '*is true*' merely expresses one's agreement with the statement in question, rather than attribute any mysterious attribute to it. Similarly, the expression '*is false*' does not attribute the quality of falsity to a statement, but expresses one's disagreement. This approach appears to prevent or dissolve the raising of the classical problem of the nature of truth. If in attributing truth or falsity to a belief I merely assert or deny the belief, the words '*truth*' and '*falsity*' become redundant. We could '*describe*', '*explain*', '*assert*', '*deny*', '*prove*', '*disprove*', '*agree*', *and* '*disagree*' exactly as we do now without using the words '*truth*' or '*true*'.

This advantage of the redundancy theory is, however, illusory, since it totally fails to prevent or dissolve the problem of what makes a true statement true, or under what conditions do we say that a statement is true or false. But we certainly need a theory of truth in the sense that we must have definite criteria of agreement or disagreement with assertions made by others and also have definite rules for making assertions ourselves. It seems to me that in the case of factual statements it is precisely the correspondence theory, which gives, the best-generalized answer to the question as to what makes a true statement true, or any statement either true or false. Both when we say that; '*London is the capital of UK*', and when we say that; '*It is true that London is the capital of UK*', we imply (in the first case implicitly and in the second explicitly) that the sentence or statement is not merely a supposal or a logical relation between ideas, independent of their factual existence, but also that it asserts an actual situation or states of affairs. We further imply that the sentence or statement is true because, in some sense or other (which it may be hard to specify or pinpoint), the statement corresponds or agrees with the actual situation. In the case of logico-mathematical statements the coherence theory gives the best-generalized answer. But both break down when they claim exclusive validity or claim to define the essence of truth, or (in the contemporary idiom) claim to provide us with a Paradigm applicable in all contexts of knowledge and truth. Like the words '*good*', '*right*', '*just*', the word '*true*' does not stand for an univocal property or essence, but is used in different contexts for different purposes. No single use can claim to be '*the true use*' or meaning of '*truth*' or '*true*', or in other words, no single theory of truth can claim to describe the essence of truth.

The above irenic linguistic approach to the problem of truth has been followed by John Wisdom and is very fruitful, indeed. But it may be extended to the existentialist approach of thinkers like Kierkegaard and Jasper's. The concepts of correspondence, coherence, utility are important for understanding the different uses of the word 'true. But equally important is the concept of authenticity, which is the key concept in the spheres of morality and religion. In these spheres the criterion of truth can be neither correspondence, nor coherence, nor utility, but authenticity or authentic subjectivity, as distinguished from verifiable objectivity. Kierkegaard or Jasper's concept of authentic subjectivity avowedly lacks logical or factual proof and implies commitment without coercive evidence. It also implies the possibility of plural objects or foci of commitment. But there is no harm in holding that in those areas of morality and religion where no factual truth claims are involved, truth means authentic subjectivity. Authenticity is inseparable from sincerity or truthfulness, but it is not reducible, without remainder, to sincerity. A person cannot be authentic without being sincere or truthful, but he can be sincere without being authentic. Authenticity is the highest form of sincerity as well as the deepest level of knowledge, since it implies self-knowledge, which, in turn, implies the plumbing of the deeps of the human self. The exploring of the deeps of the unknown self-comprising, layer upon layer, half-formed mute whisperings and intimations from mans authentic depths is a perilous task, indeed. Heroic is the person who can claim to have reached the shores of authenticity. But even he who does arrive is, forthwith, lost again in the dark depths of his individual existence, since authenticity can never be possessed as a trophy, but must be won afresh every moment of our existence. Authenticity is like the sky, which eludes us the moment we reach it. Truth, in the sense of authentic subjectivity, is the most precarious and slippery foothold for the seeker. But if he despairs of the venture and abandons the quest of this facet of truth, because it cannot be verified or established in the scientific sense, he fails to cultivate the spiritual dimension of life to the optimum degree. His self does not grow in the many splendored fullness of its potential being.

It seems to me there is no harm if the search for truth (in the sense of authentic subjectivity) leads to unverifiable (in the scientific and logical sense) plural truths, provided two conditions be satisfied, first, the seekers agree to differ, and secondly, they are moved by the will to become authentic beings rather than the will to believe.

Essay 2

A Linguistic Analysis of the Problem of Sense Perception

Introduction

The problem of sense perception together with the theory of sense data was one of the most hotly debated philosophical issues of British and American philosophy in the first quarter of the 20th century. Eminent thinkers like Moore, Russell, Broad, Price and others grappled with issues relating to the nature and relationship of sense data with physical objects and the external world. In this paper I shall try, first, to state how the philosophical problem of sense perception arises and the different lines of solution to the problem before Wittgenstein arrived on the scene. I shall then very briefly explain the rationale of the Linguistic Analytical approach to philosophical problems and theories in general. Having done so, I shall apply, in some detail, the linguistic analytical approach to the theory of sense data. This will be followed by some concluding remarks to round off the paper.

Commonsense Realism and the Statement of the Problem

According to commonsense, physical objects like chairs and tables and the entire panorama of nature exist independently of being perceived by any mind, and the act of veridical perception reveals the objectively real qualities of physical objects. Illusions and hallucinations of different types do occur, but this an aberration of normal sense perception. *Commonsense Realism* is quite satisfactory for all practical purposes. What then are the difficulties, which the philosopher notes, and which prompt him to formulate the different theories of perception?

We believe we perceive objects directly and non-inferentially. But our actual perception is confined at any moment of time to a part of the visible surface of the object rather than the whole object in the literal sense. It may be said that what we perceive directly and non-inferentially may not be the whole object, but it is after all a part of the same. But the occurrence of illusions and of plural perspectives raises the following difficulty. An optical illusion is not a case of mis-perception due to carelessness or lack of training on the part of the subject. The content of the illusion persists no matter how careful or how repeated the act of perception. The observer clearly and directly sees something as given to ones sense organs and the determinate features of the given data differ from the independent physical object. If, for example, what we directly perceive is something with an elliptical shape, this something cannot be deemed to be a part of a known circular object, like a penny. Again, if what is directly and clearly perceived has a crooked shape this something crooked cannot be a part of a straight stick. This something, which, is directly and immediately perceived in a single act of perception, has been called the *sense datum*.

It may be said that though in the case of illusions the sense data may not be equated with the parts of the physical object, this is the case in veridical perception. Since, however, the perceptual process and perceptual assurance are common in both veridical and non-veridical perception (involving one particular sense organ) how can we justify the belief that sense data are literal parts of physical objects in the case of veridical but not in the case of non-veridical perception.

If the reports given by different sense organs fail to converge, this suggests that one or the other sense organ is giving a non-veridical report. But if we concede this, we will also have to concede the basic theoretical possibility that some other test or tests might not confirm

Essay 2: A Linguistic Analysis of the Problem of Sense Perception

the perceptual report now accepted as veridical. Consequently, all that we can say with absolute certainty is that something, which is not of our own making or choice, is the *sense datum* rather than the whole object. Whether the *sense datum* is part of the physical object is a matter for inquiry, and cannot be taken as a settled matter of fact as one is certain about the sense data, as such. Philosophers thus thought that the concept of sense data was a neutral concept, which did not presuppose any theory of the universe apart from the view that our sense organs gave us reports about some independent data. The concept of *sense datum* left them free to determine the exact nature of sense data as direct objects of perception without committing them to any further ontological or epistemological theory. They retained the fundamental commonsense belief that something external to the perceiving subject exists independently of sense perception, but they questioned the commonsense view that sense perception provided a reliable photographic copy of the real world. This line of thinking was facilitated by a growing knowledge of the physiological basis of perception, which science showed to be a highly complex psycho-physical process instead of being a simple or purely mental or physical phenomenon.

DIFFICULTIES IN THE SENSE DATA THEORY:

This concept immediately raises the problem of the relation between the sense data and the physical object, indeed the very existence of the latter. If the commonsense position raises prima facie puzzles about the objects of direct perception, the sense data theory raises puzzles about the relation between sense data, as the direct objects of perception, and physical objects, as posited by commonsense as well as Newtonian Physics and Cartesian metaphysics. It is as if the cure of jaundice led to the onset of paralysis.

At the commonsense level we believe that the immediate object of direct visual perception is a part of the total physical object, just as the hand rest of a chair is part of the chair. But could sense data be said to be constituent parts of the physical object in the above sense? No, since sense data vary according to the internal and external conditions of the perceptual act, while physical objects have relatively fixed and stable constituents, according to both commonsense and Newtonian Physics. Now different sense data cannot all be the parts of one and the same object. Secondly, sense data are by the definition mind dependent, according to some philosophers, while the physical object exists independently. Now entities, which are at least partly dependent upon the mind and which, therefore, exist only intermittently cannot be a pat of a relatively permanent and independent physical object.

I think both the above difficulties could have been removed in either two ways, (a) by accepting that sense data have not merely epistemological primacy over the physical object but also ontological primacy, that is, sense data are the primary entities that constitute the *ultimate furniture of the world*, (b) the term *'sense data'* does not stand for or refer to any entity over and above physical objects, but is only an abbreviated expression for the full descriptive phrase/expression, *'physical object or a part thereof as it appears to a particular observer at a particular point of time'.*

The Neo-Realists did adopt the first half of the solution and declared that physical objects are logical constructions out of sense data. But then another problem was generated. There were different types of sense data themselves. Clearly, a double image or after image was as much a *sense datum*, in the literal sense, as a mirror image, but there were obvious differences between them. Now, if we believed in the existence of physical objects in the realist sense, we could say that there were two types of sense data namely those, which were parts of the physical object, and those, which were not parts as such. Since the Neo-Realists gave ontological primacy to sense data and held that physical objects were logical constructions, they had no criterion left for distinguishing between all manner of countless sense data that constituted the furniture of the universe. Thus, the Neo-Realists produced another puzzle in their efforts to solve the puzzle of the relation between sense data and physical objects.

It appears the Neo-Realists fell into the trap because they confused

Essay 2: A Linguistic Analysis of the Problem of Sense Perception

the reality of the perceptual experience qua experience with the reality of the object as such. The illusion is a *real* occurrence just like veridical perception. But this does not mean that the experienced datum is itself real. The Neo-Realists did not analyze the different uses of ordinary words and went about constructing a conceptual model of the perceptual situation, no matter how startling to commonsense, provided it could enable them to solve the puzzle of the relationship between physical objects and sense data. Perhaps they thought that if scientific theories could take such extreme liberties with commonsense concepts and beliefs, philosophical theories could also do likewise. But they ignored the fact that scientific theories were subjected to the discipline of empirical verification, while philosophical theories did not have this built in check, and thus could go wild.

It may be said that the futility of the speculative excesses of the Neo-Realists, on the one hand, and the honest puzzlement of Moore about the proper analysis of indubitable judgments on the other, conspired to bring the focus of enquiry upon philosophical method rather than Epistemology or Ontology. Moore had accepted the concept of sense data because of its promise of solving the difficulties created by the occurrence of illusions, and fragmentary perception etcetera and also because the concept seemed to be clear, non-controversial or non-speculative in character. But when he asked how was the *sense datum* related to physical objects whose independent existence he could not doubt, he got bogged down into insuperable difficulties, which he had the moral and the intellectual courage to admit. He never believed in a therapy that cures the disease but kills the patient. It was Moore's honest puzzlement and the honest admission that he was stuck up both in ethics and epistemology that stimulated and paved the way for Wittgenstein's linguistic analysis (much after his earlier *Tractatus*) and much different from the method of Russell's logical atomistic analysis.

Essay 2: A Linguistic Analysis of the Problem of Sense Perception

BRIEF EXPLANATION OF THE LINGUISTIC ANALYTICAL APPROACH TO PHILOSOPHICAL PROBLEMS:

According to the school of Linguistic Analysis philosophical controversies arise when we, quite unknowingly, use words and expressions in different senses and thus land ourselves in puzzles and perplexities that seem to be insoluble. For example, one may say that if nothing happens without God's will, why should criminals be punished for their crimes? This question may trigger a debate that never ends because no one is able to clinch the issue. The reason is that there is no prior agreement about the exact meaning and use of words and expressions used in the controversy, such as Creator, Divine Will, crime, justice and so on. All words of a natural language have fluid uses and meanings in different contexts.

There is yet another major source of confusion in our thinking and reasoning; our natural tendency to think that all meaningful words that are grammatical nouns must be names for some existent or entity of some kind or other. For example, noun words such as '*justice*', '*love*', '*truth*', '*government*', '*Indian Navy*', '*winter*', '*forest*', '*storm*', and so on, must refer to some specific entity or states of affairs constituting reality. Linguistic analysts maintain that this unconscious assumption generates philosophical puzzlement and controversies that can never be solved through abstract reasoning or argumentation.

Let us suppose we accept the above basic approach of Linguistic Analysis. The question now arises: Will accepting this approach suffice, by itself, suffice to clear up the mess created by numerous philosophical theories since the dawn of language and systematic reasoning in human society? The answer is a plain and emphatic no. What is further needed is the rigorous and sustained application of this type of linguistic analysis of the numerous problems of philosophy and of life, as such, with a view to pointing out in detail the origin and genesis of various conceptual illusions generated by specific semantic confusions, assumptions, Paradigms, analogies and the like. Russell or Moore did

Essay 2: A Linguistic Analysis of the Problem of Sense Perception

not practice this type of analysis. Both rejected and outgrew the classical assumption that metaphysics was the ultra-scientific anatomy of reality, while natural science dealt only with phenomena.

Is classical metaphysics, then, merely a language game and nothing more? I hold that the metaphysical quest, leads to a critical existential interpretation of the human situation and this brings about inner integration and peace of mind to the individual. John Wisdom himself points out that metaphysical theories draw our attention to unsuspected facets of human experience even though they also mislead us. This paradox of human language makes him say that the proper method of doing philosophy is *eirenics*, not polemics. We must strive to show how different theories simultaneously illuminate and mislead. Thus, for example, we must show how or in what sense the view that human willing is *free*, and the view that human willing is *determined* are both true and also false in some sense or other. The same remarks apply to the view that there is purpose in the universe and the view that there is no purpose of the universe. Contrary theories become acceptable when one asserts them as true and in the same breath qualifies them to point out how they mislead. This joint affirmation and negation reveals the complexity of the universe and the limitations of human communication. This type of dialectical reasoning is not required in the case of scientific theories because they can be empirically verified.

THE LINGUISTIC ANALYSIS OF THE THEORY OF SENSE DATA

How does linguistic analysis of the problem of perception resolve the difficulties of common sense realism without the introduction of the concept of sense data? Let us examine in some detail the argument from illusion, which is supposed to provide the grist to the mill of the theory of sense data, and let us concentrate on the well-known illustration of the stick, which is seen as bent when it is placed in water.

The sense data philosopher wants to know what precisely is the direct and immediate object of our perception when we see the stick

Essay 2: A Linguistic Analysis of the Problem of Sense Perception

in water. It cannot be the stick, since what we see, and see most clearly and directly, is bent, while the stick is straight. But we do see something. This something is the *sense datum*, which cannot be a part of the object, since the *sense datum* is bent or crooked, while the parts of the stick are all straight.

Now the linguistic philosopher points out that the way in which the sense data philosopher poses the problem is most misleading, and that if we look at the commonsense view carefully, no problem or puzzle arises. In both cases of seeing the stick outside water or inside water we see the straight stick. In the latter case we see a straight stick, part of which is above water and part of which is inside water, and the immersed part appears to be bent or crooked. We know that often things appear to have features, which they do not, in fact, have or do not appear to have the features, which they in fact have. But this does not constitute any problem, and is merely a feature of our experience, which we should take note of and accept as a given fact.

The statement that in the above case we do not see the stick but only the sense data is just the initial blunder, which vitiates our entire way of looking at the matter. The concept of sense data is introduced because we use the word, *'see'* in both the cases. If we had used the word see in the first case and the word *'appears'* in the second, there would be no trouble at all.

What is the puzzle or problem in the statement that we see a straight stick, which appears to be crooked in that part which is immersed in water? Similarly, what problem or paradox is there in the statement that an object is round or ten feet high, but appears to be elliptical or only ten inches high from such and such a distance?

The trouble only arises when we say that while the stick is straight the sense data of the stick or what we directly see is bent or crooked, or, while the penny is circular, its *'sense datum'* is elliptical. There would be no trouble if the philosophical expression; *'the sense datum is elliptical'* is avoided and we continue using the ordinary expression the penny appears elliptical. This would suffice to give us a clear and

Essay 2: A Linguistic Analysis of the Problem of Sense Perception

consistent conceptual picture of the perceptual situation without recourse to sense data language. Even using the expression *sense data* would not create any mischief, if it were understood, that *sense data* is just a philosophical expression for referring to a physical object or part thereof and not a noun to designate any new entity, that was unsuspected by the common man but discovered by some philosophers.

The term *sense datum* would then mean the *'physical object or part thereof, as it appears to the sense organs of a perceiver in a particular situation'*. The point of introducing this long descriptive phrase would be that the ordinary expression physical object and the long descriptive phrase in question do not have the same connotation, although they have same denotation or refer to the same entity, just as the expression; *'the present Prime Minister of India'* and *'the daughter of J.N. Nehru'* had different connotations but exactly the same denotation at a certain point of time. A linguistic analysis of the words *'appears'* and *'is'* removes all confusion. For example, the sentence; *'the penny is circular, but appears to be elliptical'*, makes perfect sense. Again, *'the penny is circular, but the appearance of the penny is elliptical'* is also correct. But in the second case the word *'appearance'* has been used as a noun and this suggests that it referent must be some entity or object. But whereas the word, *'is'* entails existence or predication (among several other uses) the word *'appears'* does not refer to sheer existence of something but also to an act of *'perceiving'* or a process. The moment the act stops the word appearance ceases to be applicable any more. In other words, the something to which the word *'appearance'* is supposed to refer is not an independent object but refers to an intermittent relationship involving three terms; subject, object, and act of perceiving. If so, no contradiction is involved if the object is ten feet high but its appearance is only ten inches high.

The appearance of an independent object is not another independent object, but how the subject perceives the object in non-veridical perception. We may say that the physical object consisting of parts exists independently. This independent object, at times, becomes the object of perception. When this happens its parts may be called sense data. We can also say without any theoretical difficulty that in one

Essay 2: A Linguistic Analysis of the Problem of Sense Perception

sense the sense data are parts of the physical object as such, without involving the subject, and, in another sense, they are part of the perceptual situation of the subject during the act of sense perception. When there is no observer there are no sense data in one sense, but in the other sense the sense data of an object are co-terminus with the object as such. In this sense the philosophical expression *'sense data'* becomes almost equivalent with the ordinary language expression *'physical object'*.

The point in introducing the expression, *sense datum* is that it can function as an abbreviation for the rather lengthy and cumbersome expression; *'a physical object or part thereof as it appears to an observer in a specific situation'*. Thus, we can say that a circular physical object exists all the time whether it is perceived or not, but the circular object appears as an ellipse or the elliptical *sense datum* exists only at a particular time. This type of *appearance* is however, different from mal-functional *appearances* that arise due to some reason or other but can be prevented from occurring. The *sense datum*, in the case of an optical illusion, however, persists no matter how careful the act of perception and how repeatedly the observer attempts to get at the *real thing*. In this sense the *appearance* is a hard fact of life.

But when we say that appearance is a hard fact, what we mean is that the *appearing* is a fact, and not that the contents of the appearance correspond with the contents of the world. The appearance is *presentationally* real though not *objectively* real. Thus, all we are justified in claiming is that there are many uses of the word *appearance*. In some contexts the appearance is not fleeting or arbitrary, but is a function of definite rules of perspective.

Let us further examine the logic of *'appears'*. The sense data philosopher takes a fancy for the word *'is'*. Instead of saying that, *'the penny is red but appears to be brown'* he prefers to say, *'the penny is red but its sense datum is brown'*. Similarly, he says that the *sense datum* of the stick is straight, but the *sense datum* of the stick in water is bent. The divergent sense data cannot be parts of the same object. But this difficulty is partly similar to the difficulty that the thing remains the

Essay 2: A Linguistic Analysis of the Problem of Sense Perception

same, and yet its shadow waxes big or small at different times. This phenomenon remains intriguing so long as we do not understand the laws of light and optics, but once we do come to know them, we are not mislead or deceived by the changing shapes or sizes of the shadows of a stable physical object.

The phenomenon of mirror images, double images and after images is also one of the sources of the sense data controversy. We know that mirror images are neither just like physical object not just like mental images. Mirror images cannot be touched but they are seen and can be photographed. They can certainly mislead the unwary and they play havoc with birds or animals, which cannot discriminate them from physical objects.

The argument from mirror images for the existence of sense data parallels the argument from illusion. That which is seen when we see a mirror image is not the physical object, which is on this side of the mirror, while the something seen is on the other side. That something is the *sense datum*. Now what is the difficulty in saying that a mirror image partly resembles and partly differs from both of them? As regards the relationship between the mirror image and the physical object it may be said that the mirror image is the image of the object on the surface of the mirror but this '*on*' is different from the sense of '*on*' when the book is on the table. The reasons for this is that the image is projected or formed as much behind the mirror as the object is in front, and yet looking directly on the mirror is necessary for seeing the image behind the mirror. If we focus our attention behind the mirror, in the literal sense, and not on the mirror, we will not see any image at all. The image is, thus, *sui generis* and to call it mental is as misleading as to call it a physical object.

Let us now examine some further aspects of the puzzle whether we do or do not perceive physical objects directly or only sense data are directly perceived. It is true that physical objects like, chairs and tables are not fully perceived in one perceptual act but require a number of perceptual acts from different angles and sides to make the perception complete. Our perception is avowedly partial or fragmentary. But this does not imply that our perception is indirect. We may, if we like, indicates this feature of our perception by saying that we perceive sense data directly and we perceive physical objects indirectly. But such language becomes extremely misleading, indeed.

What, if any, are the conditions in which the statement; *'we perceive sense data directly and physical objects indirectly'*, would have been true in the non-trivial sense? This statement would have been significant in a profound sense if we could point out to some perceptual experience which is direct and immediate, and in contrast with which the perception of physical objects could be held to be indirect. The sense data philosopher thinks that the experience of sense data is such a direct or privileged perception. But we find that this is not the case, and perceiving a physical object and perceiving a *sense datum* is the same type of experience and the same process, even though there is some distinction between how the different expressions are used. When I say, *'I lend you this book'*, while handing it over to you, and when I say, *'I present this book'* while handing it over, the process of handing the book is the same. Now, the point is that the process of seeing a *sense datum* or seeing a physical object is the same, although our expectations and subsequent behavior differ in some though not all situations, when I say *'I see a brown patch'*, and when I say *'I see a table'*. But because of this difference in some cases, it does not follow that the act of seeing sense data is different from seeing a table or chair. We just cannot give a clear and positive sense to the expression *'direct perception'*. And the expression *'indirect perception'* remains an empty phrase. Seeing the mirror image of a chair or seeing a chair enclosed in a glass chamber etcetera, could be deemed to be cases of indirect perception of the chair in contrast with normal perception of the chair. But normal perception of a chair itself cannot be deemed to be indirect, when there is no direct perception to contrast with.

There is, thus, no contrast of direct/indirect knowledge of physical objects and knowledge of sense data. If I say, *'I see a brown surface over there'*, and if I say, *'I see a table over there'*, in both cases I report what I directly see or confront and not what I infer, predict, dream, or remember. In point of directness, immediacy and even the certainty

Essay 2: A Linguistic Analysis of the Problem of Sense Perception

that some '*not-self*', as object, is confronting myself, as subject, there is no difference between the two perceptual situations. But does this mean there is no difference at all between the two statements? No, there is a difference.

The difference between the two statements lies in the degree of their specificity of truth claims rather than in their objective referents. Austin's example of the difference between kicking Jones door and kicking painted wood is illuminating. In other words, statements about physical objects need greater and more varied tests for confirming them, while statements about sense data do not need the same tests for their confirmation. The same feature could be expressed by saying that statements about physical objects are more vulnerable than statements about sense data. Suppose a person claims that he has intense pain in his hand or head but shows no signs of it at all. We will be justified in inferring that he is joking or lying. If, however, he persists in claiming that he does have pain sensations, but that he has the capacity to bear them with a smile on his lips, it would be difficult for us to refuse him. On the other hand, if a man claimed that there was a table over there, but the table was visible to none, could be touched by none, would support no light objects on its surface etcetera, we would be justified in referring his claim and refuting his statement. In the same manner verification procedures of statements about physical objects and statements about sense data partly differ. The sentence, '*I see a brown patch over there*' entails far less than what the sentence, '*that is a table*' entails. This latter sentence entails such truth-claims statements as, '*if you touch it, your hand will have such and such sensation*', '*if you walk in that direction or try to put another table in that region, there will be a collision*', and '*if you place a book or ash tray on the surface they will remain supported*', etcetera. On the other hand, a sentence like '*I see a brown patch over there*' entails very little.

The more the scope or complexity of the principal truth-claim the greater is the risk of its being false. On the other hand, the verification of each sub-claim tends to confirm the truth of the principal claim. But the fact is that even the truth of all the sub-claims does not logically prove the truth of the principal claim. It is logically possible

Essay 2: A Linguistic Analysis of the Problem of Sense Perception

for the principal claim to be disconfirmed by the nth test or in the nth instance, though right up to the n^{-1} instance, all sub-claims had been converging upon the truth of the principal truth claim. This is the real point behind the statement that our knowledge of physical objects is indirect, while our knowledge of sense data is direct and immediate. But then to put this point in terms of direct and indirect perception is extremely misleading indeed.

The upshot is that there is some difference between statements of the form *I see a brown patch* and of the form *I see a brown table*: but the difference is not such as the sense data philosophers suppose it to be, and this difference does not imply that our knowledge of physical objects is indirect or imply that our knowledge of physical objects is indirect or inferential while that of sense data direct and immediate. The inference of fire from the sight of smoke or the inference of a motorcar from the engine sound is indirect knowledge as compared with actually seeing the fire or the car. But when we see the fire or the car as such, knowledge cannot be said to be indirect, inferential and dubitable, though of course it is contingent. Moreover, even the knowledge of sense data is dubitable and liable to be mistaken not only in the trivial sense of being given a wrong label or name, but in the more serious sense that the sense data may be misunderstood due to carelessness or lack of training etcetera. It is, therefore, very misleading to contend that while the existence of sense data is indubitable, the existence of physical objects is only probable, or, to contend that, the reasons for the belief in the existence of physical objects are not as compelling or cogent as are the reasons for the belief in sense data. This suggests that the belief in physical objects could have been more compelling or could have possessed a higher certainty than it actually does have. But then just as in the case of indirect perception, there must be a positive sense of direct perception to act as a foil for indirect perception; there must be a sense of complete certainty in contrast with which we could understand incomplete or near certainty.

It may be said that we do have the concept of logical certainty, which we attribute to mathematical and logical truths. This is indeed the model or Paradigm of certainty, which the sense data philosopher

Essay 2: A Linguistic Analysis of the Problem of Sense Perception

has in mind or which rather holds his mind captive, as Wittgenstein aptly puts it. The philosopher forgets that the model, at least in principle, should be applicable to the belief concerned. If the model is inapplicable, in principle, to the domain of the truth-claim in question it will not make any sense to demand that its level of certainty should be the same as logical certainty. There would be no point in the lamentation that the belief in question lacks certainty. This is precisely the error into which the philosopher falls. It just does not make sense to say that a factual truth-claim should be certain in the logical sense of certainty.

The factual model of certainty is quite different from the logical model. Indeed we could even say that factual certainty and logical certainty are distinct concepts, which are clumsily lumped together due to our general tendency to ignore subtle differences and seek unity in variety. This is the craving for unity or the search for essences in the language of Wittgenstein. Consequently, if factual truth and logical truth are different concepts, each with its own appropriate reach or area of application, the demand for logical certainty in an area where it is not applicable, by definition, is like the demand that ethical judgments be verifiable like the scientific, or that the general laws of science or other law-like truth-claims be confirmed like particular truth-claim of the type, *'this cat is on the mat'*. The demand for this type or model of certainty is rooted in our tendency to suppose that the word *'certainty'* must designate or stand for some essence of certainty behind all cases or instances of real certainty.

When however we free ourselves from one particular model of certainty, that is, the logical, we realize that in the area of factual truth-claims the demand for this particular model is misplaced. We, then, no longer feel prompted to say that the existence of physical objects is either not certain, or less certain than that of sense data. We do not feel prompted to say that while we have direct and immediate knowledge of sense data we have indirect knowledge of physical objects. Thus the puzzle of the relationship between physical objects and sense data and other related philosophical problems are not generated at all. This constitutes their dissolution instead of their solution (in the classical speculative or analytical tradition).

CONCLUSION

The above linguistic analysis of the theory of *sense datum* has removed some of the confusions that arise in our thinking due to our almost inevitable tendency to reify words specially those that are used as nouns in our discourse. This creates artificial problems that demand true answers or solutions when in fact there is no problem and no true answer that excludes other answers. This means that the so-called *philosophical problem of perception* and the so-called *sense datum theory* to solve the problem were both pseudo arguments. At the same time the expression *sense datum*, as a philosophical or theoretical construct, had a limited use as a convenient short hand expression for the much longer expression, '*the physical object or part thereof as presented to the observer at a particular space-time moment*'. Genuine factual knowledge relating to human perception involving different human sense organs and the nervous system and the human subject as such lies in the domain of anatomy, physiology and psychology rather than of logic or philosophy. Wittgenstein has clearly stated that linguistic analysis does not add anything to our knowledge but just dissolves our confusions or illusions that give birth to the different theories of perception or knowledge or ethics or metaphysics as the case may be. The proper way to acquire knowledge is to tap the door of factual knowledge or to investigate the truth according to the scientific method. However, the removal of confusions and logical errors is, by itself, no mean achievement. In fact, it amounts to human liberation from artificial theoretical perplexity.

The above linguistic analysis of the problem of perception also shows very clearly the value of John Wisdom's concept of the *paradox of linguistic communication*. This is the paradox that all acts of communication illuminate as well as mislead the *communicatee*. Thus, to say that '*one perceives physical objects indirectly*', or to say that '*physical objects are logical constructions out of sense data*', or to say that '*physical objects are nothing but permanent possibilities of perception*', or to say that '*all perceptual knowledge is confined to our own perceptions*' and so on, at one and the same time, are penetrating remarks that make a valid point but also mislead in specific ways. In what follows I shall

Essay 2: A Linguistic Analysis of the Problem of Sense Perception

give several examples of this paradox in different theories of perception and knowledge.

The sense data theory draws our attention to the different ways in which words are used and different types of truth-claims are verified. It also helps us to understand the logic of our language when we deal with different types of nouns, verbs, adjectives or prepositions even when they are grammatically the same. The realization that though the grammatical structure of the sentence, *'this rose is red'*, and the sentence, *'this rose is beautiful'*, is exactly the same, their functional logic and methods of verification are entirely different. The uses or functions, implications and methods of verification of words and expressions that refer to physical objects, individuals, corporate bodies and processes and so on are all different. These issues are barely understood or known at the common sense level of the users of ordinary language.

According to the *Representative Realism* of Descartes and John Locke the primary qualities of matter, namely substance, shape, size, location and motion are objective and inhere in the external world independently of being perceived by any observer or not, while the secondary qualities, namely color, taste smell and sound are subjective and they appear only when the external substance impacts some human percipient in the act of perception. The secondary qualities do not inhere in the external world but emerge when the object and the perceiving subject are suitably placed. The Phenomenalist approach to knowledge and the external world holds that both primary and secondary qualities refer to reality as it appears to some subject, but one has no access to *Reality* as it is by itself. All such views or theories have some *'point'* to them, but none is free from some objectionable inner twist or knot. In other words, each theory illuminates and misleads at the same time. Locke's theory appears impregnable so long as we operate in the Newtonian universe of space, time and motion. But it seems to break down when some one begins to question the objectivity of space and time as such. Indeed this is what Einstein did. Kant had done it much earlier. Phenomenalism is, perhaps, logically irrefutable. On this view even the most accurate and rigorous factual knowledge based on the scientific method becomes tainted by human subjectivity.

Essay 2: A Linguistic Analysis of the Problem of Sense Perception

The objective idealist position is hardly a clear statement and can be interpreted in diverse ways. Moreover, there is no compelling or logically coercive support for accepting it. However, both the phenomenalist and idealist positions are logically possible though they cannot be established or *clinched*. The same applies to Realism as a theory of knowledge.

The upshot of the above linguistic analysis is that the demand to prove any of the above philosophical theories of knowledge and of Reality is misconceived. This is the case not because of any limitation in our powers of reasoning, or the scientific method. It is due to our asking wrong questions because of semantic confusions in regard to the nature, types and functions of human language in action. This was Kant's point of departure. Despite his tremendous genius, the Western world had to wait for almost two centuries before Wittgenstein could formulate his mature views on the diverse functions of language and his key concept of *language games* to bring out the hidden nature of pompous and forbidding philosophical theories which can never be proved or disproved one way or the other.

To conclude, if theories such as Realism, Phenomenalism, at bottom, be alternative language systems or games, that are neither true nor false, but only helpful or illuminating (in part) and misleading (in part) why not play the game of ordinary language and avoid technical philosophy as such. This is what the famous Oxford thinkers, J.L. Austin and Gilbert Ryle recommend. All said and done ordinary language is not more misleading/illuminating than philosophical theories. Moreover, we are all familiar with its standard expressions, unlike the pompous expressions philosophers love to coin, every philosopher taking delight and pride in ones own theories or '*isms*'.

APPENDIX 1
ABOUT THE AUTHOR

Jamal Khwaja was born in Delhi in 1926*. His ancestors had been closely connected with the Islamic reform movement, inaugurated by Sir Syed Ahmad Khan, the founder of the famous M.A.O. College, Aligarh in the second half of the 19th century, and the Indian freedom movement under Gandhi's leadership in the first half of the 20th century. After doing his M.A. in Philosophy from the Aligarh Muslim University, India, he obtained an honors degree from Christ's College Cambridge, UK. Later he spent a year studying the German language and European existentialism at Munster University, Germany. At Cambridge he was deeply influenced by the work of C.D. Broad, Wittgenstein and John Wisdom, apart from his college tutor, I.T. Ramsey who later became Professor of Christian Religion at Oxford. It was the latter's influence which taught Khwaja to appreciate the inner beauty and power of pure spirituality. Khwaja was thus led to appreciate the value of linguistic analysis as a tool of philosophical inquiry and to combine the quest for clarity with the insights and depth of the existentialist approach to religion and spirituality.

Khwaja was appointed Lecturer in Philosophy at the Aligarh Muslim University in 1953. Before he could begin serious academic work in his chosen field, his family tradition of public work pulled him into a brief spell of active politics under the charismatic Jawahar Lal Nehru – the first Prime Minister of India. Nehru was keen to rejuvenate his team of colleagues through inducting fresh blood into the Indian National Congress.

---
* Jamal Khwaja was born in Delhi on August 12, 1926. However, most official records mistakenly show 1928 as the year of birth.

Appendix 1: About The Author

He included young Khwaja, then freshly returned from Cambridge, along with four or five other young persons. Khwaja thus became one of the youngest entrants into the Indian Parliament as a member of the lower house from 1957 to 1962. While in the corridors of power he learned to distinguish between ideals and illusions, and finally chose to pursue the path of knowledge rather than the path of acquiring authority or power. Returning to his *alma mater* in 1962, he resumed teaching and research in the philosophy of religion. Ever since then Khwaja has lived a quiet life at Aligarh.

He was Dean of the Faculty of Arts and was a member of important committees of the University Grants Commission and the Indian Council for Philosophical Research before retiring as Professor and Chairman of the Department of Philosophy in 1988. He was a frequent and active participant in national seminars held at the Indian Institute of Advanced Study, Shimla.

His works include, *Five Approaches to Philosophy, Quest for Islam, Authenticity and Islamic Liberalism, The Call of Modernity and Islam, Essays on Cultural Pluralism, Living The Quran in Our Times, The Islamic Vision of Sir Syed* (in Urdu) and several articles and essays. He was invited to deliver the Khuda Bakhsh Memorial Lecture at Patna. He was one of the official Indian delegates at the World Philosophical Congress Brighton, UK, in 1988, and also at the International Islamic Conference Kuala Lumpur, Malaysia, in 1967, and the Pakistan International Philosophy Congress, Peshawar, Pakistan, in 1964. He has visited the USA and several countries in Western Europe.

He performed Hajj in 2005.

APPENDIX 2
SELECT BIBLIOGRAPHY

The following is a list of important books and articles that have helped to shape the thinking and the meta-philosophical orientation of the author. It is far from being a complete survey of the literature. The following abbreviations have been used:

Schilpp.   *The Library of Living Philosophers* edited by P. A. Schilpp.

M.   *Mind, A Quarterly Review of Psychology and Philosophy*

P.   *Philosophy*

P.P.R.   *Philosophy and Phenomenological Research*

P.R.   *Philosophical Review*

H.J.   *Hibbert Journal*

P.A.S.   *Proceedings of the Aristotelian Society*

A.S.S.   *Proceedings of the Aristotelian Society*, Supplementary Volume.

BOOKS

Ayer, A. J.	*Language, Truth and Logic*, Second Edition. London, 1946.
Broad, C.D.	*Critical and Speculative Philosophy, In Contemporary British Philosophy*, First Series, edited by Muirhead, London, 1924.
Brock, W.	*Contemporary German Philosophy*, Cambridge, 1935.
Bochenski, I.M.	*Contemporary European Philosophy*. Berkeley. 1950.
Barnes, W.H.F.	*The Philosophical Predicament*, London, 1950.
Dewey, J.	*Reconstruction in Philosophy*, N.Y. 1948.
Dewey, J.	Article on 'Philosophy', in *Encyclopedia of the Social Sciences*.
Emmet, D.M.	*The Nature of Metaphysical Thinking*, London, 1945.
Feigl, H.	*Logical Empiricism in Twentieth Century Philosophy*, edited by D. D. Runes, N.Y. 1947.
Findlay, J.N.	Article on '*Phenomenology*', in *Encyclopedia Britannica*
Hodges, H.A.	*The Philosophy of Dilthey*, London, 1944.
Heinemann, F.H.	*Existentialism and the Modern Predicament*, London, 1953.
Heidegger, M.	*Existence and Being*, London, 1949.
Jaspers, K.	*The Way to Wisdom*, Yale, 1954.
Lazerowitz, M.	*The Structure of Metaphysics*, 1955.

Appendix 2: Select Bibliography

Macintyre, A. (Ed)   *Metaphysical Beliefs*, Illinois, 1957.

Malcolm, N.   *Moore and Ordinary Language*, in Schilpp, Moore, N.Y. 1942.

Murphy, A.E.   *Whitehead and the Method of Speculative Philosophy*, in Schilpp, Whitehead, N.Y. 1951.

Moore, G.E.   *A Defense of Common Sense*, in Contemporary British Philosophy, Second Series, 1925.

Russell, B.   *Logical Atomism*, in Contemporary British Philosophy, First Series, 1942.

Ryle, G.   *The Theory of Meaning in British Philosophy at Mid Century*, edited by C.A. Mace, London, 1957.

Ryle, G.   *The Concept of Mind*, London, 1949.

Ratner, J.   *Dewey's Conception of Philosophy*, in Schilpp, Dewey, N.Y. 1951

Reichenbach, H.   *The Rise of Scientific Philosophy*, Berkeley, 1951.

Ramsey, I.T.   *On the Possibility and Purpose of Metaphysical Theology*, in *Prospects for Metaphysics*, edited by I.T. Ramsey, London, 1961.

Toulmin, S.E.   *Place of Reason in Ethics*, Cambridge, 1950.

Urmson, J.O.   *Philosophical Analysis*, Oxford, 1956.

Waismann, F.   *How I see Philosophy*, in *Contemporary British Philosophy*, Third Edition, ed. by H. P. Lewis, London, 1956.

Appendix 2: Select Bibliography

Wittgenstein, L. *Tractatus Logico-Philosophicus*, London, 1922.

Wittgenstein, L. *The Blue & Brown Books*, Oxford, 1958.

Wittgenstein, L. *Philosophical Investigations*, Oxford, 1953.

Warnock, G. J. *English Philosophy Since 1900*, London, 1958.

ARTICLES

Ayer, A. J. *Does Philosophy Analyze Common Sense*, A.S.S., 1937-38.

Burtt, E. A. *Generic Definition of Philosophical Terms*, P.R., 1953.

Burtt, E. A. *The Problem of Philosophical Method*, P.R., 1946.

Berlin, I. *Logical Translation*, P.A.S., 1949-50.

Black, M. *Linguistic Method in Philosophy*, P.P.R. 1947-48.

Black, M. *Metaphor*, P.A.S., 1954-55.

Broad, C.D. *Some Methods of Speculative Philosophy*, A.S.S. 1946-47.

Conger, G.P. *Method and Content in Philosophy*, P.R., 1946.

Copleston, F.C. *Possibility of Metaphysics*, P.A.S. 1949-50.

Copleston, F.C. *Function of Metaphysics*, P, 1953.

Daitz, E. *The Picture Theory of Meaning*, M, 1953.

Evans, J.L. *On Meaning and Verification*, M. 1953.

Farrell, B.A. *An Appraisal of Therapeutic Positivism I & II*, M. 1946.

Appendix 2: Select Bibliography

Farber, M.	*Function of Phenomenological Analysis*, P.P.R. 1940-41.
Jaspers, K.	*Importance of Nietzsche, Marx & Kierkegaard in Philosophy*, H.J. 1951.
Hahn, L.E.	*Metaphysical Interpretation*, P.R. 1952.
Hahn, L E.	*Starting Point of Metaphysics*, P.P.R. 1957-58.
Hampshire, S.	*Fallacies in Moral Philosophy*, M. 1949.
Hampshire, S.	*Logical Form*, P.A.S. 1947-48.
Macdonald, M.	*Linguistic Philosophy and Perception*, P. 1953.
Macdonald, M.	*The Philosopher's Use of Analogy*, P.A.S. 1937-38.
Malcolm, N.	*Are Necessary Propositions Really Verbal*, M. 1940.
Murphy, A.E.	*Two Versions of Critical Philosophy.* P.A.S. 1937-38.
Nowell-Smith, P.H.	*Philosophical Theories,* P.A.S. 1947-48
Pepper, S. C.	*Metaphysical Method*, P.R. 1941.
Paul, G. A.	*Is There a Problem about Sense-data,* P.A.S. 1936-37.
Rogers, D. W.	*Philosophic Method*, P.R. 1947.
Ryle, G.	*Taking Sides in Philosophy*, P. 1937.
Ryle, G.	*Ordinary Language*, P.R. 1953.
Ryle, G.	*Knowing How and Knowing That*, P.A.S. 1945-46.
Ryle, G.	*Systematically Misleading Expressions*, P.A.S. 1931-32.

Appendix 2: Select Bibliography

Ryle, G. et al *Symposium on Phenomenology,* A.S.S. 1931-32.

Stern, G. *On the Pseudo-Concreteness of Heidegger's Philosophy,* P.P.R. 1947-48.

Stace, W.T. *Metaphysics and Experience,* P.P.R. 1948-49.

Stace, W.T. *Phenomenology and Metaphysics,* P.P.R. 1949-50.

Strawson, P.F. *Wittgenstein's Investigations,* M, 1954.

Stevenson, C.L. *Persuasive Definitions,* M. 1938.

Stevenson, C.L. *Emotive Concept of Ethics,* P.R. 1950.

Werkmeister, W. *Seven Theses of Logical Positivism, I & II,* P.R. 1937.

Warnock, G.J. *Metaphysics in Logic,* P.A.S. 1950-51.

Wisdom, J. *Metaphysics,* P.A.S. 1950-51.

Wisdom, J. *Metaphysics and Verification,* M. 1938.

Wisdom, J. *Philosophical Perplexity,* P.A.S. 1936-37.

Weitz, W. *Oxford Philosophy,* P.R. 1953.

INDEX

A

a priori knowledge, 26, 30
Absolute Spirit, 31, 35
adaptation, 44
aesthetic statements, 86
aesthetic value, 45
Agnosticism, 28, 30, 88, 92, 94
agreement, 2, 5, 6, 14, 24, 36,
agriculture, 37, 44, 45
ambiguous, 9, 56
analogical thinking, 39, 49
analogy, 15, 39, 49
analysis, 3, 11, 16, 17, 24-27, 29, 32, 40, 47, 48, 51, 52, 53, 55-62, 64, 66, 67, 71, 72-81, 85, 86, 92, 93, 95, 96, 98, 99, 102-105, 111, 115, 123, 127-129, 131, 138, 140, 141
analytical approach, 25, 32, 51-53, 58, 62, 66, 74, 76, 88, 103, 104, 123, 128
animism, 45
antinomies, 93
anti-thesis, 31
apologetics, 16, 90, 91
appearance, 19-21, 23, 29, 31, 48, 110, 112, 131, 132
applicable, 15, 45, 49, 113, 115, 116, 118, 120, 131, 136, 137
aptness of a metaphor, 49
Aristotle, 2, 52
art, 3, 9, 33, 34, 36, 38, 46

assumptions, 5, 6, 11, 22, 24, 26, 32, 36, 60, 61, 65, 78-80, 128
atomic facts, 58
atomic propositions, 58, 60
attack, 12, 47, 106
attitudes, 62, 84, 87, 88, 90, 93, 103
authoritarian religion, 10
authority, 7, 10-17, 58, 91, 142
autonomy, 16
Ayer, A. J., 61, 74

B

Barth, Karl, 91
Being, 13, 19, 41, 60, 63, 69, 91, 95-99
belief system, 10-13, 20
bewitchment of intelligence, 73, 98, 103
Bradley, F.H., 52-54, 58
Brunner, Emil, 91
Buddhism, 10

C

categories of understanding, 25, 31, 97
central problem of philosophy, 88, 97

149

certainty, 24, 43, 67, 93, 115, 125, 134, 136, 137
Christianity, 10, 13, 84, 91
circular approach, 30
class conflict, 35
cognitive, 26-29, 42, 62-65, 73, 74, 106, 107, 110, 113, 116
commitment, 7, 10, 11, 14-17, 38, 83, 84, 91, 95, 96, 120
common sense beliefs, 54, 55, 58
communication, 5, 101, 129, 138
Comte, 52
conceptual analysis, 11, 48, 104, 105
conceptual evolution, 42, 45
conceptual field, 2-6, 13, 23-27, 31-32-37, 40-46, 81, 101-102-106
conceptual figure, 42
conceptual model, 46, 127
conceptual reconstruction, 12
conceptual unification, 38, 40, 49
conciliation, 71
consistency, 11, 49, 54, 58, 105
constructional concept of knowledge, 23
contemporary, 2, 4, 6-7, 17, 39, 47, 52-53, 80, 92, 101, 111, 113, 120
contextual, 24, 26, 29, 61, 64, 99
controversy, 2, 6, 10, 25, 29-30, 50-51, 56, 67, 88, 113, 117-118, 128, 133
conventional definitions, 80, 81
Coue, Emile, 76
creation, 5, 13, 41, 91

criteria of truth/validity, 1, 25, 37, 48
cultural anthropology, 34
cultural conditioning, 36, 50, 104
cultural gestalt, 34, 35, 36
culture of human awareness, 107
culture, 5, 35, 37, 38, 40, 42, 45, 106, 107

D

Darwin, 44
Descartes, 2, 26, 27, 79, 89, 90, 139
descriptive contexts, 46, 49
despair, 30, 39, 48, 88, 121
destructive skepticism, 30
Dewey, John, 3, 35, 36, 52, 99
dialectical approach, 23, 30, 31
dialectical laws, 31
Dilthey, 3, 35, 36, 99
directional analysis, 60, 61
disagreement, 3-6, 11, 21, 25, 28, 29, 50-57, 61, 66, 75-78, 80, 102, 106, 107, 119
discipline, 47, 79, 85, 97, 127
discord, 17
discovery, 10, 23, 26, 31, 47, 80, 81, 98
distortion, 46, 79
dread, 95-99, 104
Dualism, 24, 64, 78, 85

E

economy of human life, 84
eidetic, 78, 81
emotive, 62, 64, 73, 74, 110, 113, 116
Empiricism, 29, 109, 111
epistemological theory, 23, 26-31, 64, 87, 90, 110, 114, 115, 125, 126
error, 15, 21, 39, 102, 137, 138
essence, 5, 27, 58, 68, 71, 78-81, 86, 88-90, 95, 98, 109, 116-117, 120
ethical statements, 47, 49, 55, 64, 74, 76
ethnocentric, 43
Eucken, 35
evaluation, 37-39, 81, 84
evil, 4, 5, 13, 42, 83
exhortation, 48
existential analogy, 38, 39
existential choice, 39
existential import, 32
existential unification, 38, 39, 40, 78
Existenzerhellung, 86, 87, 92-94, 103
experience of reality, 80
explanation, 3, 21, 30, 33, 38-41, 44, 63, 83, 127
external, 38, 39, 40, 78

F

factual discourse, 34, 49, 65, 117
faith, 12, 14, 15, 38, 40, 84, 87, 90, 91
fallacy of independent location, 22
fallacy of simplism, 107
false, 22, 31, 36, 37, 46-49, 62-64, 67, 74, 99, 110-111, 116-119, 129, 135, 140
feeling, 34, 37, 39, 62, 70, 93, 99, 107, 114
Fido-Fido theory of, 71, 72, 109
field, 2-6, 13, 23-37, 40-46, 50, 61, 76, 81, 88, 101-106, 141
field-blindness, 104
forms of human understanding, 27
freedom, 4, 16, 17, 47, 95, 103, 141
Fromm, Erich, 10
functional analysis, 104, 105
functions of language, 32, 61, 66, 140

G

generalization, 70, 72
Germany, 34, 141
gestalt, 34-36
Ghazzali, 6
gliding philosopher, 94, 105
God, 13, 40, 41, 83-85, 89, 91, 128
grammar, 2, 73, 81, 105
ground of sensible appearance, 31

H

Hahn, 61
harmony, 6, 7, 11, 17

Hartmann, 32, 79, 92
Hedonism, 85
Hegel, 23, 30-35, 53, 91, 101
Heidegger, 87, 88, 92, 95-100, 103
Heinemann, 95, 98
helplessness, 39
hidden assumptions, 26, 32
historical situation, 3-5, 36
Historicism, 35, 101
history of philosophy, 77, 101
horticulture, 44
Humanism, 78, 105
humanistic religion, 10
Hume, David, 2, 53, 54, 65, 87
Husserl, Edmund, 52, 53, 78, 80, 81, 96
hypothesis, 39, 42, 70, 91

I
Ibn Arabi, 13
Ibn Rushd, 6, 13
Idealism, 24, 35, 42, 64, 69, 78, 94, 105
ideology, 35
illuminating, 15, 16, 29, 34, 37, 39, 89, 95, 99, 106, 110, 113, 118, 135, 140
illusion, 21, 32, 53, 73, 98, 112, 123, 124, 127-129, 132-133, 138, 142
immanent Ontology, 78
immanent, 5, 16, 17, 20, 24, 47, 48
imminent death, 94
important nonsense, 60

improper question, 46, 71, 72
incarnation, 13
incomplete symbol, 59
infallibility, 13, 14, 15
inner attitude, 87
instinct, 58
integration, 32, 83, 105, 129
intellectual autonomy, 15, 16
internal, 12, 113, 126
interpretation, 13, 16, 32, 33, 38, 40-42, 44, 70, 78, 79, 88, 95, 99, 104, 112, 129
intuition, 28, 78, 112
intuitionism, 29, 109
investigation, 1, 14, 28, 66, 97, 106
irenic approach, 74, 101, 120

J
James, William, 52, 118
Jaspers, Karl, 9, 87, 88, 92-95, 98, 103, 104, 107, 120,
judgment, 4-6, 14-16, 27, 38, 40, 44, 70, 79, 85, 98, 106, 112-117, 137
juxtaposition of views, 94

K
Kant, 2, 6, 9, 24-32, 52-53, 65, 69, 78, 87, 92, 94, 103, 139-140
Kierkegaard, 85, 87-92, 95, 120
knowledge, 6, 19-33, 38, 44, 52, 63, 69, 73, 79, 84, 88, 93-94, 99, 106, 109-117, 120, 125, 134-142

Index

L

language game, 111, 129, 140
language trap, 73, 80, 100
Lebensphilosophie, 35
Leibniz, 27, 51-53
leitmotif, 12, 36, 38, 51-52
limit-situations, 94
linguistic analysis, 26, 29, 48, 53, 57, 66, 71-74, 77, 99, 103, 105, 123, 127-131, 138, 140-141
linguistic, 24, 26, 29, 47, 48, 53, 57, 62, 64, 66, 71-81, 95-107, 120, 123, **127-131**, **138,**, **140**, 141
Locke, John, 2, 139
logic of language, 71, 73, 76
Logical Atomism, 57, 58, 60, 95
logical positivists, 3, 28, 33, 53, 62, 64, 73-74, 93, 102-103
logical uncertainty, 50
logico-mathematical inference, 15
longing for truth, 30

M

magnet, 40
manifold, 5, 6, 31, 34, 41, 70, 75, 105
Mannheim, Karl, 5, 105
Marcel, G., 87, 95, 107
Marx, Karl, 3, 35, 87-88, 106
Materialism, 24, 35, 42, 64, 78, 85
Mathematics, 1, 3, 24, 27, 51, 53, 58, 61, 67, 84, 88, 115, 117
mind and matter, 95

meaningful, 31, 40, 59, 62, 64-65, 68-69, 71, 94, 109, 128
meaningless, 62-65, 68
meanings, 9, 57, 61, 66, 70, 75, 76, 128
measurement, 70
mechanism, 24, 29
meta-empirical facts, 80
metaphilosopher, 2, 6, 47
meta-philosophy, 1-4, 29-32, 40, 54, 78, 92
metaphysical, 6, 9-13, 19-25, 28, 30-34, 39, 40, 42, 46, 52-53, 57-58, 61-65, 73, 75, 78, 86, 88, 91-103, 110, 129
metaphysics, 2, 19, 26, 27, 29, 32-34, 42, 53, 58, 60, 63, 65, 73, 78, 87, 88, 82, 94-99, 102, 103, 106, 110
meta-science, 1, 2
methods of investigation, 61
modality, 72
modes of mystical experience, 28
modes of verification, 62, 64, 115, 116, 139
molecular facts, 58
Monadism, 51
Monism, 24, 51, 64, 78, 85
Moore, G.E., 3, 53-60, 66, 74-77, 95, 97, 102, 107, 123, 127-128
moral choice, 16
mother –field, 104
multi-cultural, 17
Mutazalite, 13

Index

N

Napoleon, 45
natural science, 1-3, 20, 33, 37, 65, 72, 79, 84, 93, 129
Naturalism, 35
nature of philosophy, 4, 17, 77
nebulous, 56
negation, 72, 96, 99, 129
Neurath, 61
Nietzsche, 3, 87, 88, 92, 95
Nihilism, 29, 30
Nowell, Smith, 64, 73, 74
Nominalism, 69
Nothing, 95-99
Noumena, 25, 29, 31, 110

O

object of knowledge, 27
objectively true, 26, 46, 48
ontological approach, 25, 27, 99
ontological, 24-31, 40, 42, 52, 69, 85, 87-90, 94-99, 103, 125-126
Ontology, 19, 32, 33, 78, 79, 96-98, 102-105, 127
optimism, 39
organic evolution, 44
organism, 34, 38, 44
out-field, 105

P

pain, 4, 13, 29, 42, 45, 135
Pantheism, 47
paradigm use, 69, 71
paradigm, 4, 29, 52, 69-74, 77, 106, 110-112, 115-118, 120, 128, 136
paradox, 57, 66, 67, 70, 77, 99, 102, 129, 130, 138, 139
peace, 11, 17, 45, 129
perception, 20-23, 27, 38, 86, 93, 112, 123-136, 138-139
perceptual apparatus, 22
perceptual, 20-28, 37-39, 55, 79, 111, 112, 124-127, 130-135, 138
personality needs, 104
perspective, 21, 86, 94, 104, 124, 132
Phenomenology, 52, 78, 79, 81
Philosophers, 2-7, 10-17, 20, 23-26, 30, 32, 35-36, 39, 42-47, 51-57, 64, 66-67, 70, 73, 75-77, 80-83, 86, 88, 92-93, 97, 99-109, 124-126, 129-137, 140.
philosophical anthropology, 81, 92
philosophical disagreement, 3-5, 21, 51, 61, 76, 80, 106, 107
philosophical interpretation, 38, 40, 70, 104
philosophical investigations, 66
philosophical perplexity, 47, 50, 67, 71
philosophical system, 47, 48
philosophical theory, 45, 47, 67, 75, 77, 110
physical objects, 54, 70, 77, 86, 89, 123-127, 133-139
Physics, 3, 33, 79, 125, 126
Plato, 2, 5, 6, 26, 27, 46, 52
Platonic design, 45
Pluralism, 24
poetry, 33, 37-40, 49, 110

polemics, 71, 101, 129
politics, 35, 114, 141
Polytheism, 45
portrait, 45
Positivism, 27, 29, 35, 52, 61, 63, 64, 72, 110
postulates, 28, 112
poverty, 2, 41
power, 35, 39, 41, 45, 140-142
practical ethics, 86
pragmatic fruitfulness, 49, 105
Pragmaticism, 52
prediction, 38
prescriptive statements, 64
problems of men and of philosophers, 36
Procrustean, 32
proof, 14, 15, 50, 70, 90, 91, 115, 120
pseudo, 38-40, 62-65, 90, 93, 100, 105, 138
Psychoanalysis, 47
Pure Forms, 79
pure movement, 69

Q

question, 1, 5, 13, 21-32, 36, 46-49, 54, 56, 61-68, 71, 72, 75, 76, 95, 96, 105, 109, 113, 114, 118, 119, 128, 131, 137, 139

R

Ramsey, 77, 141
Rationalism, 13, 29, 85, 109, 111, 112
Realism, 21, 22, 27, 69, 123, 124, 129, 139, 140
recommendatory use of language, 80
reconstruction of concepts, 11, 26
refraction, 28, 46
regulative ideas of pure reason, 28
reification, 59
relativity, 22, 25, 27
religion, 2, 7, 9, 10, 14, 16, 33-38, 46, 87, 91, 110, 118, 120, 141, 142
religious approach, 7, 9, 10-20, 100-102
Richards, I.A., 74
rules of use, 105
Russell, Bertrand, 3, 53, 54, 57-63, 71-72, 77, 95, 102, 123, 127, 128
Ryle, Gilbert, 140, 47, 66, 71

S

Saint Augustine, 90
Saint Peter, 10
sanctum sanctorum, 88
Sartre, 87, 88, 95, 96, 102, 103
Scheler, Max, 3, 35, 81, 92
Schelling, 30
Schleiermacher, 90
Schlick, 61
science, 1-3, 20, 21, 27, 32-38, 42, 44, 49, 51, 58, 61, 63, 65, 72, 79, 88, 90, 95, 96, 97, 106, 110, 111, 115, 118, 125, 128, 137
scientific explanation, 33, 39

Index

scientific method, 2, 48, 49, 51, 52, 63, 64, 93, 138-140
sense-data, 5, 55, 77, 123-139
sensible reality, 29
simplicity, 22, 49, 53, 55, 105
situation, 2-6, 21, 22, 36, 44, 45, 51, 52, 100, 101, 104, 107, 114, 116, 119, 127, 129, 130-132
situational analysis, 104, 105
situational determination, 5, 35
situational matrix, 3, 25, 34, 37
skepticism, 28, 29, 30
social organism, 34
Sociography, 34
Sociology, 34
Socrates, 9, 10, 83, 102
sources of disagreement, 75
spectrum, 10
speculation, 11, 12, 20, 21, 53, 57, 61, 83, 88
speculative approach, 10, 78
Spinoza, 2, 9, 10, 27, 46, 51, 52
sruti, 12
Stern, G., 100
Stevenson, 64
striving, 39, 90
suffering, 40
super-science, 42, 79, 110, 27, 32, 33, 49, 63, 65, 88, 95, 106
super-structure, 35
Supreme Being, 13, 91
symbol, 62, 72
syntax, 59, 105
synthesis, 31, 85
synthetic statements, 27, 31, 53, 62, 69, 80

T

Taoism, 10
technical questions, 86, 90
technique of analysis, 80, 86
Das Umgreifende, 94
Theism, 24, 35, 47, 64, 94, 105
theologian, 7, 12, 17, 83, 90
Theology, 90, 91
theory of language, 80
theory of meaning, 25, 63, 65, 72, 74, 76, 80
thesis, 31
tools, 46, 84
Toulmin, Stephen, 73, 74
Tractatus Logico Philosophicus, 58, 61, 66, 72, 102, 127
transcendental Ontology, 33, 78, 79, 102, 103
transcendental, 17, 20, 24, 26, 33, 47, 65, 78-80, 94, 102, 103
true, 2, 7, 24-26, 28-31, 36, 37, 45-49, 54-57, 62-65, 67, 68, 69, 73, 74, 77, 83, 85, 89, 91, 94, 98, 99, 109, 110-113, 116-120, 129, 133, 134, 138, 140
truth, 1, 3, 6, 11-13, 16, 23, 25, 28, 30, 32, 33, 37, 40, 43, 45-48, 50, 54-56, 59-61, 64, 72, 80, 84-86, 91, 95, 97, 98, 101, 102, 104, 106, 109-121, 128, 135-139
trans-empirical, 49, 68, 79, 80
triad, 31, 32
Troeltsch, 35
truth, 1, 3, 6, 11-13, 16, 23, 25, 28, 30, 32, 33, 37, 40, 43, 45-48, 50, 54-56, 59-61, 64, 72, 80, 84-86, 91, 95, 97, 98, 101, 102, 104, 106, 109-121, 128, 135-139

truth-claim, 40, 48, 60, 64, 110, 111, 116, 117, 120, 135, 136
truth-function, 59
truth-value, 59
type mistake, 59, 71
type of discourse, 3, 25, 39, 40, 52, 59, 62, 64, 65, 71, 72, 76, 80
typology of discourse, 63, 65

U

uncertainty, 50
understanding, 17, 25, 27, 31, 35, 56, 60, 62, 72, 81, 89, 97, 99, 120
unification, 38, 49, 78, 81
universe, 4, 5, 9, 19-21, 38, 39, 41, 44-46, 49, 85, 93, 94, 125, 126, 129, 139
unverifiable, 53, 63, 121
Upanishads, 12

V

valid, 7, 15, 29, 36, 99, 104-106, 114, 115, 138
validity, 1, 5, 11, 15, 16, 24, 26, 28, 32, 36, 48-50, 52, 63, 65, 81, 91, 92, 94, 101, 114, 116, 120
value judgment, 6, 98
value systems, 11, 17, 35, 47, 50, 104
values, 7, 16, 36, 42, 58, 81, 83, 86, 90, 116
variations, 44, 64
Vedas, 12
verifiable, 38, 46, 48, 49, 62, 93, 116, 120, 121, 137

Vienna Circle, 53, 61

W

Waismann, 61
Warnock, 61
Weltanschauung, 33
Whitehead, A.N. 22, 32, 79, 105
willing, 34, 39, 90, 107, 129,
Wisdom, John, 47, 58, 66, 78, 95, 99, 103, 110, 111, 120, 129, 138, 141
Wittgenstein, 3, 47, 58, 60, 61, 66, 67, 70-78, 98, 100, 103, 107, 111, 123, 127, 137, 138, 140, 141
World Spirit, 31
world views, 36-38, 43, 45, 47-49
world-orientation, 92, 93

Z

Zeno's paradox, 70

More information about the Author
and his various works can be found at the Author's website

www.JamalKhwaja.com

Get FREE Downloads of Essays & Articles by the Author

Or, visit

www.AlhamdPublishers.com

www.ingramcontent.com/pod-product-compliance
Lightning Source LLC
Chambersburg PA
CBHW021149080526
44588CB00008B/275